# MICHAEL HONE

## *Court Homosexuality during the Reign of*

# LOUIS XIV

**Coffee-Table Edition**
**8.5 X 11 inches**
**21.59 X 27.94 cm**

*Cover painting: Marc'Antonio Pasqualini Crowned by Apollo, 1641,*
*by Andrea Sacchi*
*Homoerotic art during the time of Louis XIV*

*All pictures are in the public domain*

© 2022

**My books include:**

*Cellini; Caravaggio; Cesare Borgia; Renaissance Murders;*
*TROY; Greek Homosexuality; ARGO; Alcibiades the*
*Schoolboy; RENT BOYS; Roman Homosexuality; Renaissance*
*Homosexuality; Homoerotic Art [in full color]; Sailors and*
*Homosexuality; The Essence of Being Gay; John [Jack]*
*Nicholson; THE SACRED BAND; German Homosexuality;*
*Gay Genius; SPARTA; Charles XII of Sweden; Mediterranean*
*Homosexual Pleasure; CAPRI; Boarding School*
*Homosexuality; American Homosexual Giants; HUSTLERS;*
*Omnisexuality, the Death of Gay and Straight Sex; Y.M.C.A.*
*Homosexual Haven; All-Boy Porn Stars; All-Male*
*Pornography; VINTAGE The Golden Age of All-Male Erotica;*
*Sebastian; The History of British Homosexuality; The History*
*of Homosexuality in the Armed Forces; 1970s The Glorious*
*Age of Male Eroticism; 1980 The Final Years of the Glorious*
*Age of All-Male Eroticism; Alexander VI; All-Male Film*
*Masterpieces; All-Male Pornography; Astorre Manfredi; The*
*Bell Époque; The Bloomsbury Set; Saint Bartholomew Day*
*Massacres; Buckingham; Cicero; Louis XIII; Directors' Cut*
*The Filming of All-Male Erotic Masterpieces; Edward II,*
*Exploration Giants; Elagabales; French Homosexuality; Five*
*Renaissance Wonders; Florence; The Garden of Allah;*
*Alexander and Hephaestion; Hollywood's Homosexual History;*
*Homoerotic Couples; Homosexual Warriors; Homosexual*

*Heroes; Homosexual Athletes; Julius II; Love the Gay Way; Male Bonding; Male Nudity; Male Self-Pleasuring; The All-Male Porn Industry; The Mattachine Society; Menshikov; Homosexuality in Greek Mythology; The History of Orgies; Phallus; The Roaring Twenties Homosexual Heyday; Homosexual Secret Societies; The Trojan War; Tasmania; Vasari; Venice; Vintage Erotica; Wash West; Today's Homoerotic Film giants,* **and others.**
**I live in the South of France.**

## DEDICATION

**As a youth of 18 I discovered Versailles at the side of an art professor and guide, thanks to whom I am today French and have spent my entire life in France. It is to this ambassadress, Suzy Fromenti, the most important person in my life, that this book is dedicated.**

# CONTENTS

# INTRODUCTION

Louis XIV, like the Ancient Romans, was a believer in war, war that united citizens behind a cause, that kept the people on the battlefields and not behind barricades in revolt, that brought wealth and luxuries through conquest, and extended a country's borders, for the greater the nation the more powerful its king.

Louis XIV's brother Philippe d'Orléans was homosexual, and how Louis XIV escaped the same destiny is a mystery because he had lived through the combination of three ingredients that would normally have created the perfect storm: in first place, he was raised by a mother who adored him and whispered in his ear, from the maternal bed they shared, that his reign was a direct gift from God, a message reinforced by the women in whose apartments he grew up--aunts, nieces, grandmothers and female servants; secondly, his father Louis XIII preferred men, an example often followed by sons; and lastly, Louis XIII died when Louis, the future Louis XIV, was five, the absence of a boy's natural pilot a recurrent cause of homosexuality. We must always keep in mind that the categories homosexual, heterosexual and bisexual did not exist at the time, although libertines--free-thinkers who lived lives of *varying* amorous impulses--did.

Born in Saint-Germain-en-Laye and raised in the Palais-Royal in the center of Paris, Louis grew up through a series of revolts called *Frondes*, mobs infuriated by taxes, hard living conditions and little parliamentary representation, one of which forced entry into his bedchamber, his mother holding him to her as the crowd assured itself that the boy was alive and well, for French kings were adulated and believed to possess even curative powers. But the indelible memory of the assault branded the child throughout his entire life, a frozen dagger lodged forever in a ventricle of his heart, the reason he abandoned Paris, with its easily-barricaded streets, for the open and defensible fields of Versailles, the reason he built an indomitable army and headed it with loyal generals and marshals of historic repute.

Born on the 5th of September 1638, his mother Anne of Austria's homosexual husband Louis XIII had taken 23 years to impregnate her--encouraged, believe some historians, by his lover

Luynes present during the proceedings, while others believe the child was fathered by a long list of candidates that historians have drawn up over the past four-hundred years, even if Anne's preference may well have been women, or at least one woman, Luynes' wife Marie (3). Called Louis Dieudonné, the baby was indeed a gift of God, one that not only assured France a crown prince, but the foremost heterosexual prince in French history, engendered through the assumed loins of the foremost homosexual in French history, Louis XIII (37).

Anne became regent on Louis' demise, her chief minister and intimate counselor Cardinal Mazarin, who replaced Richelieu at Richelieu's death, Mazarin whom a number of Louis' biographers believe had secretly married the queen, and was one of the candidates cited as being Louis XIV's father. Pierre Séquier was her chancellor, another Richelieu protégé, a triumvirate that jailed all opponents from within parliament and the nobility. Opposition in the form citizen-backed *Frondes* rose-up, revolts supported by Louis XIII's brother Gaston, by the Condés, the Contis, the Rohans [one member of which was Queen Anne's lover Marie de Rohan, Luyne's wife], and other dissident families such as the Soissons and that of François de La Rochfoucauld. The *Frondes* based their legitimacy on the claim that they were acting on Louis' behalf, that their enemies were Anne and Mazarin, the power of both weakened when Louis came of age on the 7th of September 1651, although Mazarin continued to direct diplomatic and financial policy until his death in 1661, after which Louis surprised the world by proclaiming that he would rule without a chief minister, stating, ''Up to this moment I have been pleased to entrust the governance of my affairs to the late cardinal. It is now time that I govern them myself. You [government officials], I order to seal no orders except by my command; sign nothing, not even a passport, without my command; to render account to me personally each day, and to favor no one.''

Louis chose Jean-Baptiste Colbert to establish order in centuries of economic chaos, which Colbert did by bring in an economic surplus in 1666, largely through *indirect* taxation, leading the people to believe, for the first time in French history, that they were being *less taxed* [an arm used to this day in France where lower-income French *pay no taxes*, while each time they buy anything whatsoever they're bludgeoned by an invisible sales tax of a whopping 20% (sales taxes in America varying from 2.9% to 7.25%)]. Up to the time of Louis XIV, kings were allowed to tax without the consent of the nobles as long as the nobles themselves were not taxed, the nobles justifying the exclusion with the argument that in times of war it was they who had to raise troops, feed and clothe them, as well as provide their weapons and horses. Only the peasants were directly taxed, taxes collected by intermediaries [dubbed tax farmers], who served themselves along the way, only a fraction of the collected taxes eventually entering the king's coffers. Reforms made tax collection more fluid and better supervised under Colbert, and the nobles, for the first time in French history, were not exempt, which decreased the burden on the poor [while the nobles nonetheless found loopholes to the new procedures, as the rich do today, many paying no direct taxes at all]. The church was obliged to turn over part of its tithes from parishioners in a tax that was euphemistically called a ''free gift'', agreed to by the pope in Rome who needed Louis in the Catholic fight against heretics, the pope calling him ''the most Christian king'', Louis who was able to keep the inquisition out of France and usher in religious peace by banning Calvinist Huguenots, a monumental transformation from the time of Louis XIV's grandfather, Henry IV, who was himself a Protestant before becoming a Catholic. Replacing free-thinking Protestants with indulgence-selling Catholics was a huge setback for France, happily corrected during the French Revolution, the Catholic church controlling 40% of France's wealth until then, the church's base the uneducated peasantry, which made up 97% of France's population in 1484, down to 80% in 1700, reduced to far less during the Enlightenment with it concept of ''equality'' and ''the freedom of the individual''.

But more importantly, Louis and Colbert encouraged French industry, the source of wealth and even greater taxes, the emphasis on manufacturing--from silk to steel to shipbuilding--which also reduced expenditures on imports. Of no less importance, the French language became the language of every civilized court in Europe.

Spain, England and the Holy Roman Empire were the great powers, Mazarin deciding to unite France with Spain through the marriage of King Philip IV's daughter, Maria Theresa, to Louis in 1660, the drawback being that Maria Theresa renounced all her claims to the Spanish throne, but because her dowry was never fully paid, France claimed the renunciation null and void. This led to interminable wars with Spain and with the Spanish Netherlands, conflagrations in which England, Sweden and the Holy Roman Empire were involved, as was Italy, at first allies with France and then France's enemies. Louis sent expeditions to today's America and Canada, gaining hold over 1/3$^{rd}$ of the continent--named Louisiana after Louis. François I had aligned France with the Ottoman Empire, a scandal at the time, an alliance confirmed by Louis who in addition established good relations with Morocco to the South and China to the East. Louis encouraged piracy as a way of stinging the dominant sea powers, England and Spain, and he decided to banish, for once and for all, Protestantism from French soil by giving heretics the choice to convert to Catholicism or to leave France, a surprising 400,000 of whom did convert, while a Catholic baptism became a requirement of all children. The Edict of Nantes, which had given Protestants the right to practice their religion (12), was replaced by the Edict of Fontainebleau that threatened them with forced baptisms, the outcome the end to the centuries-long wars of religion, as Louis promised to do in his coronation oath. Once the dust from the above had settled, French territory had been expanded to include Alsace, and French borders extended to the Rhine, both gains valid to this day.

But wars on all fronts put France in dire debt, at the same time as famine killed two million people between 1693 and 1710, worsened by armies stealing supplies directly from peasants, starving troops invading even the English island of Guernsey in search of wheat. All other European countries suffered as much, the end result of which were a series of peace treaties signed between Queen Anne of Britain, Philip V of Spain, the Holy Roman Empire, the Dutch Republic and Louis XIV.

Louis XIV

# PART I

## THE HOMOSEXUAL ROOTS TO THE COURT OF LOUIS XIV

## HENRY III

Catherine de' Medici ruled France from the time of the death of her husband, Henry II. She was the *éminence grise* under her sons François II and Charles IX, and she ruled during Henry III's years. Henry III fell to his knees before his mother and kissed her hands, and well he should. Although by far the most intelligent of his brothers, he hadn't Catherine's knowledge of state and worldly affairs. And God on high knows that, for Catherine, knowledge did not come without years of learning. Already, as a new bride, she knew there was something wrong with her physical relationship with Henry II who would daily run off into the arms of his much older and deeply loved mistress Diane de Poitiers, this despite the fact that François I, Henry's father, had been present during the wedding-night penetration, a necessity to ensure that the marriage had been consummated. Henry VIII wanted to divorce his first wife, Spanish Catherine of Aragon, saying she had slept with her first husband, Henry's brother. Catherine denied this, claiming that Henry's brother Arthur had been too ill to perform, this despite Arthur's sly-dog comment, the next morning, that he had visited, the night before, the depths of Spain. Because there had been no witnesses, years of contention followed, the result the end of Catholicism in England, replaced by Anglicism with Henry at its head. François had thusly witnessed his son deflowering Catherine, apparently noting nothing amiss going on in the shadows.

The future Henry III and his brother Charles IX, Charles shown her before he grew the moustache that covered an unsightly birthmark, a blemish the artist was instructed to omit.

Diane had taken Henry and his manhood in hand when he was but a boy, taught him to perform with her and with the girls she readied for him. He couldn't live without her, the proof the intertwining of their initials on every surface where it could be sculpted or wrought in iron. We don't know if he was as ''endowed'' as his father François I was universally known to be, but he had suffered years of imprisonment when he'd taken the place of his father, Charles V's captive in Spain, years that stunted him psychologically (3). Diane extracted him from himself, giving emotional life to that part of him that could well have otherwise perished.

**The portrait of one of François' two big attributes, his nose. Court ladies sought his help in releasing them from their noisome virginity, although not all appreciated his royal command to open their legs, one married victim who had her husband infect himself with syphilis so that she could infect the king, while another slashed her face, which did not deflect François because it was not her face that interested him. Captured in battle by King Charles V, he was released when his two sons took his place as hostages, traumatizing the future Henry II.**

Catherine, wishing to know what hold Diane had over him, had a hole drilled into the floor that gave onto Diane's rooms. Alas, we don't know what she saw, but it wasn't what she and Henry had been doing. She changed her ways, the consequence the birth of child after child after child, her love for Henry II limitless.

She loved her son Henry III at least as much. He had his *crise d'adolescence,* adolescent ups-and-downs, when he turned to Protestantism, calling himself the Little Huguenot, Huguenot the French word for Protestant. He forced his sister Margot to give up Catholic prayers and prayer books, until he later turned against Protestants, eventually leading a siege against them at La Rochelle, a Protestant holdout. He was instrumental in their destruction during the St. Bartholomew Massacre in 1572, during which Protestants were not only slaughtered, but denuded, their privates cut off, their anuses violated, the worst desecration on French soil until the French Revolution of 1789 (12). The catalyst for his change of heart had been his mother, Catholic Catherine, who reigned him in when she felt his anti-Catholicism had gone far enough.

The origin of the word Huguenot is too disputed to interest us here. In France they numbered around two million during the time of Henry III and were inspired by the writings of Jean Calvin. Those forced to flee the country at one period or another went mostly to the Netherlands, England, Ireland, Scotland, Sweden, Switzerland and, for total independence, America, where they founded New Rochelle. A Protestant ship made it to Cape Town and two others, carrying 500 souls, to an island off today's Rio de Janeiro where they built Fort Coligny as a defense against natives. When finally overpowered, they were obliged to either convert or face death, most preferring to die for their faith. Expulsed by Louis XIV, they ultimately gained equality after the French Revolution, thanks to the Declaration of the Rights of Man and of the Citizen in 1789.

**Diane de Poitiers and her name linked to Henry's**

Religious unrest in France had begun under François I. Ideas from Luther and from Calvin were spilling over into France and François at first tried to be tolerant. But when the Protestants began to placard Paris with anti-Catholic heresy, he ordered the first burnings at the stake in 1535, followed in 1545 by the massacre of Mérindol where thousands were killed by his troops, the end of the wars in 1598, the dead numbering 3 million by then.

By 1562, during the reign of Henry II, there were 2 million Calvinists, one of whom was the mother of Henry de Navarre, himself a Protestant until he became the King of France, Henry IV, converting to Catholicism by proclaiming that Paris was well worth a mass.

Henry de Navarre, future Henry IV, changed from Catholic to Protestant and back when politically expedient, a heterosexual who fathered homosexual Louis XIII, who engendered, after 23 years of effort, Louis XIV, France's most homophobic king, so desired he was called Louis-Dieudonné, Louis the God-Given.

Henry II was accidentally killed during a joust and his son François II, age 15, was made king under the capable guidance of his mother Catherine de' Medici. She had three alternatives: she could fight the Huguenots, although martyrdom just made them more determined; she could allow them free rein in France, causing revolts from her Catholic subjects, thereby assuring her beheading; or she could attempt negotiations, which she chose. An agreement was signed in which Catholicism was designated as the nation's religion, Huguenots given the right to freely pray, although outside the walls of towns.

But unrest continued in the provinces and in 1562 the Duke de Guise, a unbridled Catholic who hated the heretic Huguenots, arrived outside the town of Vassy where he insulted Protestants in the midst of prayer. Words turned to drawn swords and the Protestants were massacred by the duke and his troops. This inspired the Duke de Condé, a Huguenot, to seize the town of Orleans, after which other towns in other parts of France were overrun by Protestants. Furious, Catholics rose up in places like Toulouse and slaughtered the heretics.

Catherine de' Medici observing the victims of the slaughter for which she was largely responsible, known historically as the Saint Bartholomew's Day Massacre, a painting by Edouard Debat-Ponsan.

Catherine was able to bring peace through the Edict of Amboise which united Huguenots and Catholics against the English who held Le Havre, which worked until Le Havre was finally taken by the French. Charles IX came of age and both the Protestant Condé and the Catholic Guise went back to raising troops and taking towns for their respective religions. Protestant Queen Elizabeth of England entered the dance, as the French say, by sending money to the Huguenots. Charles IX was a Catholic but he greatly admired Admiral Coligny, a Protestant. Coligny came to Paris for the wedding of Margot, Charles' sister, under the protection of Charles, but was assassinated to Charles' shocked horror, an assassination orchestrated by Charles' mother Catherine. Coligny had been wounded in the face earlier during the day and was in his town residence when Guise's men entered and killed him. His body was thrown from a window, he was stripped naked and his privates were cut off, after which most Protestants would be stripped and castrated in the same way. He was cut up by the mob who hanged part of him, threw a part into the Seine, and burned the rest. Thus began the Saint Bartholomew's Day Massacre, with the slaughter of 4,000 Huguenots in Paris alone (12).

Coligny.

Orphaned at age 3, Coligny was raised by his uncle Anne de Montmorency who instructed him in martial arts and Erasmian humanism. After the massacre at Vassy he joined his cousin Louis de Condé at the head of a Huguenot army. Charles IX brought him to court where he served as his model, although Coligny's attempt to kidnap the boy and convert him to Protestantism, followed by Catherine de' Medici's warning that either Charles kill Coligny or both their heads would adorn the walls of the Louvre on the end of pikes, led directly to Charles' order to assassinate him, an assassination which ignited the powder keg that engulfed all of France.

Thinking that Henry would perhaps never become King of France, Catherine paid a fortune to have him elected King of Poland, an elective monarchy. When Charles IX died, she sent secret word to him in Cracow, telling him to return to Paris, detailing each move he was to make, nearly down to the hour. Henry, who so hated freezing Poland and its rustic setting that he hid himself away in his apartments, suddenly became the life of the party, issuing forth with his mignons--his boy lovers totally loyal to him. Originally mignon meant everything from a servant to a buddy, but due to Henry's use of them, mignon became synonymous with catamite, a designation purportedly invented by Calvinists. He gave banquets and balls, dressed to kill with his earrings and pearl-studded doublets, literally dancing the night away. The ruse worked. He was able to flee while the castle slept, his baggage and his pockets--and the pockets of his mignons--

stuffed with Polish diamonds and gems. Horses had been put aside at relays, and he crossed the border of Austria in sight of Polish troops sent to haul him back *manu militari*. There, Emperor Maximilian welcomed him like a son. Then came Venice, the city of vice, where it is believed that excessive sex led directly to his physical decline, a decline so severe that in later life it would take him days in bed to recuperate after an orgasm. He may also have suffered from syphilis. His mother met him at Lyons. He knelt before her, she the vital force of his kingship. Catherine had already tried to marry him off to Queen Elizabeth but Henry wanted nothing of her ''stale virginity'', so she tried to interest Elizabeth in Henry's younger brother, the fifteen-year-old hunchback François Duke d'Alençon, who would have perhaps won the queen's hand had France been part of the boy's dowry, which it wasn't.

Scarred by smallpox, his spine deformed, François became heir to the throne after the ascension of his brother Henry III. Rejected by all except his sister Margot, he escaped from court and joined the Protestant forces of Louis de Condé. In order to get him back, Henry III and his mother Catherine signed the Edict de Beaulieu that provided Protestant leaders with land and titles, François himself taking Henry's former title of Duke d'Anjou.

It was then suggested that he marry Elizabeth, Queen of England, and he duly went to London to meet his future bride, he age 24, Elizabeth 46. She actually took a liking to him, calling the deformed lad her ''frog'', the slang word for the French to this day. The wedding didn't go through although, quite incredibly, Elizabeth's chief advisor, William Cecil, Lord Burghley, was wholly behind the union. The French too saw the possibilities, because at the death of Elizabeth he would become King of

England. Those against the marriage, like Elizabeth's spymaster Walsingham, told her that as a Catholic, François would be responsible for a renewal of religious violence throughout England. Also incredible was the fact that François remained by Elizabeth's side from 1578 to 1581, when she bid her frog farewell.

At the head of troops François went to Antwerp, prepared to seize the city as a first step to conquering Flanders. He told the townspeople that he was there on a visit, and wished to do a little sightseeing, accompanied by his troops. The citizens agreed, and once inside the Antwerpens massacred the lot, François escaping by the skin of his teeth. His mother Catherine wrote him this loving note: ''Would to God that you had died young. You would never have been the cause of the deaths of so many brave gentlemen.''

Ill with malaria, his mother's wish came true in 1584, when François was 29.

Before the death of her son Charles IX, Catherine had found Charles a wife and approved of his mistresses, the foremost of which was an English girl named Marie that Catherine accepted when she became convinced that Marie was solely interested in Charles and not the French throne. Catherine allowed Marie to come to Paris where Henry infuriated his brother Charles by paying court to her and teaching her French. Charles got his revenge by having 50 of his troops pierce their ears and put in gold earrings as worn by Henry and his mignons, mince about, bringing down peals of laughter from everyone except Henry.

Catherine also saw to her daughter Margot's future. Like Henry, Margot was intelligent, perhaps the most intelligent of them all, and also like Henry she appreciated boys, without number, obliging her to occasionally sojourn in the country where she gave birth. Catherine had sought many matches for her but finally the choice fell on Henry de Navarre. Because he was a Protestant, Margot refused to say Yes when Catherine asked her if she would consent to the marriage. During the marriage ceremony Margot remained silent when asked if she would take Henry de Navarre for her lawful husband, a question the priest repeated three times. Finally the king brusquely came up behind her and violently pushed her head forward, shouting ''She says Yes'', the priest hurriedly pronouncing them man and wife. Henry de Navarre's mother, as a Protestant, was against her son's marriage to the Catholic Margot, whom Catherine silenced by having her poisoned days before her son's marriage (3).

Catherine tried to straighten Henry out. She organized banquets in which the girl servers were nude. Henry just yawned. The only women who caught his attention were his sister Margot and the wife he would take, in whose company Louis spent hours creating dresses for both, arranging their make-up and doing their hair.

Catherine's health had been abandoning her for years: de' Medici gout that had killed a dozen Medici leaders including the great Cosimo and Lorenzo *Il Magnifico* (2), torturous pain from bad teeth, and bad indigestion. She had kept strong through a will that defies the imagination, witnessing the intolerable loss of her sons, one after the other, begging Death to take her after each loss so she wouldn't be obliged to endure still another.

Her prayers were answered at age 67 when she passed into eternal silence, a rare force of nature shared by few men and fewer women--Caterina Riario Sforza de' Medici, Catherine of All the Russias and a non-Catherine, Eleanor d'Aquitaine (11).

Henry lacked popularity among the people due to several factors. One was his homosexuality, an offense the French would have overlooked had he produced an heir. But he didn't and the thought of what he and his mignons did together in private was simply too easily imagined and disgusting for Frenchmen to ignore. France was decidedly not Italy: the Renaissance awakening to Greek mores would never fully take hold in Paris as it did in Florence (13). Henry's grandfather François I had allowed Cellini and his lads to gallivant around Fontainebleau and Paris (1), even though François was a woman's man and sodomy was punished by burning at the stake.

Secondly, Henry cut himself off from the French people as he had isolated himself from the Poles. At the time, French kings traveled extensively from town to town, allowing the commoners to see and touch them [kings reputed to have curative powers], even defecating [discreetly] in their presence thanks to specially designed portable chairs. Henry's brother Charles, from 1564 to 1566, entered 109 towns under the Royal Arches the townspeople had set up to honor him; while in all of Henry's kingship he went to only 4. Royan had prepared for a visit that he cancelled, but Henry still requested that the people offer him the money they had set aside for the event. French kings also ate in public. Henry was obliged to do so too, but he had a barrier constructed so that no one could approach closely, to the disgust of court members, some of whom refused to attend the dinners while the barriers were up. Yet his mignons had not only unlimited access to his table, they were automatically allowed entrance to his bedroom, sexually cavorting with lads coiffed in the manner of their king, lads who wore large earrings and adorned themselves with gems and pearls as he did, and who even adopted the king's taste in lively little dogs.

Henry was so reviled by those who wished for a real king, who were jealous of the ascendance of his mignons, and those of true noble blood who couldn't stomach a king who preferred dancing to leading his army in battlefield conquests, that stories of every sort were invented, which historians are in constant quicksand when dealing with them, especially Henry's sexual pastimes, an example the rumor that his mignon François d'Espinay de Saint Luc, so jealous of two new boys the king passed the night with, told his wife that Henry was having an adventure with a certain *woman*, knowing his wife would tell the queen who would make Henry's life miserable, his gallivanting with *boys* of far less importance to her.

Many of Henry's mignons were sexually ambivalent or had strong heterosexual preferences, but allowed themselves to be coiffed and dressed by those mignons who were openly homosexual, the king's casting couch the key to a veritable cornucopia of riches, lands, titles and even one's own chateau, all thanks to money coming into the treasury through taxation. He gave one boy a gift of 100 *écus*. When the lad heartily thanked him, he upped it to 1,000. The boy nearly collapsed with gratitude, especially when Henry, pleased, increased the largess to 10,000, which perhaps inspired the same scene, later, in Molière's *Le Bourgeois Gentilhomme.*

How many boys never married because they were exclusively homosexual is not known, although most did marry, in luxurious style thanks to their king. Jean-Louis de Nogaret de La Valette, Duke d'Épernon was perhaps the love of his life, to whom he said on his deathbed: ''I assure you that I have more regrets in leaving you than you have in seeing me leave this world,'' [*Je t'assure que j'ay plus de regret de te laisser que tu n'as de contrition et déplaisante de me voir partir de ce monde*], and ''This soul that separates itself from your beautiful body'' (21).

**Épernon**

Henry's boys were rarely adventures of one night, most of his relationships woven of threads as solid as steel. He showered his lads with proofs of love, through private conversations and ''pillow'' confidences, small gifts that the lads knew would become veritable fortunes if they sufficiently demonstrated their loyalty, as well as Henry's gestures of affection by arranging a lad's hair, applying, lovingly, a touch of coloration to a boy's cheeks, verifying the cleanliness of a mignon's shirt collar. Henry was as devoted to his mignons as was Christ to his disciples, and they would literally die for him, some doing so in duels and on the battlefield, many so courageous and fearless that one wonders if they were not chosen by Henry to compensate for the feminine part of his body. One chronicler at the time stated that it was the woman in Henry that transvestized herself as a man, more than the man in Henry who transvestized himself as a woman.

One of Henry's former lovers, Louis de Bussy d'Amboise, called Bussy, had posed problem by ridiculing Henry's mignons, vaunting the fact that he, Bussy, took women from the front, unlike the mignons with each other, pushing under the carpet that he had been, at first, the favorite of Henry, whom Henry passed on to his brother François, Bussy who ended up paying with his life when waylaid by enemies, perhaps the husband of one of the numerous women he frequented (3).

**Bussy**

It was now Henry de Guise--called Scarface because of a battle wound, Guise a boyhood lover of Henry's--who was causing problems. From a very powerful family, loved by the French for his rabid anti-Protestantism and bravura, possessor of lands and chateaux of vast wealth, he was in debt up to his ears due to lavish spending and monumental losses through gambling. Just as Bussy had provoked Henry, so Guise did now, pushing Henry's mignons into duels by crudely divulging their appetites, as he or one of his followers did to Jacques de Lévis de Quélus, saying that he earned advancement through the habile use of his buttocks. When another of Guise's boys, François de Balzac d'Entragues, said to have been a beauty, similarly mocked Quélus, Quélus called for a duel. At the time duelers had seconds who assisted the duelers, although they never took part in the combat. But this time the participants, six in all, decided to join in the fun. They met at the

Horse Market. Quélus was seconded by his friends Maugiron and Livarot; Entragues by Ribérac and Schomberg. The fighting, of incredible savagery, left Maugiron and Schomberg dead on the field nearly immediately. Ribérac died a few hours afterwards and Livarot was healed enough to walk six weeks later. Quélus received 19 wounds and took 33 days to die, despite Henry's offer of 100,000 *écus* if the doctors saved him. The handsome Entragues got off with a scratch.

Jacques de Lévis de Quélus and Louis de Maugiron

One source has them dying in a kind of homosexual embrace: Ribérac projected himself against the body of Maugiron, impaling himself at the same time on Maugiron's sword, Schomberg hit Livarot on the head with the blade of his weapon at the same moment Livarot plunged a dagger into Schomberg's heart, both, interlaced, falling to the floor.

In the streets the people sang to show Entragues their support: ''Entragues and his companions trounced the mignons; it's only too bad they didn't kill more'' (14). [*Entraigues et ses compagnons/Ont bien étrillé les mignons/Chacun dit que c'est bien dommage/Qu'il n'y en est mort davantage* (21).] Entragues was named governor of Orleans in order to pacify the town, which he did in a blood bath [*le sang coulait à flot*], massacring Protestants who believed they were safe there, their bodies thrown into the Loire. The director of the University was killed by his own students, one of 1,000 victims.

A month later another of Henry's boys was waylaid and murdered, perhaps by the husband of one of his mistresses. It was said that Henry's lads always died crying out his name, but never that of God or their mothers. Henry was bedridden after each of these events, and in honor of Quélus and Maugiron he had mausoleums raised in the church of Saint-Paul, one for each--and he carried of lock of their hair with him until he himself was cut down. He personally removed Quélus's earrings that he kept in a jeweled box near him at all times.

But Henry got over Quélus's loss, and went on a sex binge. Michel Pernot tells us, from apparently reliable sources, that in 1585, in Limours, Henry and his mignons entertained 15 whores in an orgy that lasted 6 days.

Anne de Joyeuse [Anne was also a man's name], one of Henry's archmignons, was highly educated and had been introduced to war at a young age by his father with whom he fought against the Huguenots. Henry named him governor of Mont Saint-Michel and offered him Limours. When Henry's brother François died, Henry gave Joyeuse governance of Alençon and Joyeuse's brother governorship over Anjou. Joyeuse massacred 800 Huguenots at La Mothe-Saint-Héray and then attacked the Protestant forces of Henry de Navarre. Taken prisoner, the moment Joyeuse's identity was revealed he was fatally shot through the throat, at age 27. Among the other 2,000 Catholic dead on the field was his brother Claude.

Anne de Joyeuse

Épernon and Joyeuse had come to Henry's attention about the same time. Épernon, on campaign with Henry, had dressed his luxurious tents in view of the king's, adorning them with the fine horses and handsome pages, as beautifully attired as those of the late Bussy, in black velvet decorated in threads of gold. Épernon, much younger than Henry, was courageous to a fault, with willpower of forged steel, panache, and an extremely lofty opinion of himself. Avaricious, he was the ant to Joyeuse's grasshopper. Joyeuse had attracted Henry's attention thanks to his bravura, but also due to his beauty, at its most glorious when Henry laid eyes on him at age 17. At court Joyeuse was said to have had a beautiful soul in an even more beautiful body. Lovable and cheerful, he was thought to have been Henry's greatest piece of art, and, with Épernon, the most cherished of his mignons, the reason they were called his archmignons. He was well educated and could talk books with Henry, whereas Épernon was oriented towards arms. Both were Henry's personal reserves, but both could benefit from women at will, which both did. They were the only two men to have unannounced access to the kings quarters, which both used also at will. They cost the country millions in lands, jewels, residences and weddings, Joyeuse's marriage alone was said by one source to have cost 3 million *livres*, a sum it took fifteen years for the king's treasury to repay, as well as a dowry of 1 million more, making these lads by far the most expensive lays in the history of outlays. [A *livre tournois* was divided into 20 *sols* (*sous* after 1715), each *sous* divided into 12 *deniers*. An *écu* was worth 45 sous.]

After Quélus's death, historians note a complete change in Henry, who went from one excess to another. The queen had a miscarriage, a girl, and he realized that if nothing were done to encourage Heaven to give him descendants, the throne would go to his brother François, or to Henry de Navarre [the future Henry IV], both far from Henry III intellectually, even though François was smart and Henry de Navarre would later become one of France's most loved kings. In personal hygiene, too, they were unlike Henry, bathing infrequency, and Navarre was even noted, in texts, for his stinking armpits.

Henry changed his dress, adopting grays, browns and blacks. He became assiduous in his attendance of masses, took a new confessor, founded an order of knights, the Order of the Saint-

Esprit, its purpose to defend Catholicism and destroy the heresy of Protestantism. His knights were decked out in sumptuous black velvet, and the Order's ceremonies were profuse with objects of unimaginable price, like pure-gold censors. Each knight was obliged to confess at least twice a year and each received 1,000 *écus* a month, a princely sum.

When Henry failed to engender a son, he did penitence. He went to Chartres on foot, a distance of 80 kilometers [55 miles], *5 times*. Of all the nobles who accompanied him on the first pilgrimage, only Henry de Guise made it back to Paris on foot. On the 4th pilgrimage, out of 64 mignons, 14 returned and one nearly died. On the fifth he spread out over the floor of the cathedral in the form of a cross, for three hours, kissing the marble surface.

Henry and his nobles went to Notre Dame and other churches dressed in white, the cloth covering the mignons' backs, crimson from self-flagellation. Henry's mother Catherine, a true Renaissance intelligence, was aghast at the excesses, while Henry's wife, second to none in piety, could not support the sight of her husband, his head covered in a white hood, in the center of his moaning, bloodied boys.

And the people? They didn't believe for a moment what was, for them, a completely hypocritical sham. They chanted a ditty: ''Mignons who lightly bore the blood of France on their butts, were not only striking their backs but their asses too, the source of their offense'' (14). [*Mignons, qui portaient doucement/En croupe le sang de la France,/Ne battaient le dos seulement/Mais le cul qui a fait l'offense.*] Parisians were shocked by the boys in white and the flagellation, certain their king had gone mad.

He was also hated because he had the Duke de Guise murdered. Guise was an extremely popular man in France, a man who hated Protestants as did most Frenchmen, a man's man who liked wenching and the hunt, virile pursuits unknown to Henry. His popularity was such that Henry became certain Guise would topple him, especially as Guise did not want Henry de Navarre, a Protestant, to follow Henry should Henry die. In fear of his life, Henry invited Guise to his study, access to which was a long corridor. When Guise was in the middle of it, forty men, twenty from each end, entered. Guise immediately went for his sword, fought valiantly, and died of a hundred wounds. Henry ran to his mother, ''Now I am the uncontested king!'' She answered, ''No, you've just lost your kingdom.''

Henry de Guise, Scarface.

Henry formed the Catholic League as a way of putting himself on the throne in the place of frivolous boy-and-little-dog-loving Henry III, although the League's declared purpose was the eradication of Protestantism [which may have been Henry de Guise's aim at the time of its creation]. Scarface immediately received the backing of Philip II of Spain and Pope Sixtus V. The League cleverly used any natural disaster--plague, famine and massacres--as God's vengeance for French tolerance of heretics, which worked even among Protestants who, after the massacres following Saint Bartholomew Day, began to believe that God was not in their corner.

**Henry standing over de Guise by Duprat**

For all these reasons, when King Henry was assassinated the French went wild with joy. Henry had taken residence at Saint-Cloud, outside Paris, shortly after Catherine's funeral. By chance, one of Henry's officials passed a monk on foot and offered him a place in his carriage. When the monk, Jacques Clément, said he was on his way to Saint-Cloud with secret information for the king's ears only, the official took him to see Henry.

The king was at his dressing table attending to his beauty. He welcomed the monk warmly and begged him to be seated next to him. Clément was a very special monk in that he received word directly from God, the last message ordering Henry's death. Henry knew Clément had come with secret information and allowed him to lean forward and whisper it into his ear. Clément did so, extracting at the same time a dagger from his sleeve that he thrust to the hilt into Henry's abdomen. The king's screams brought the immediate entry of the guards who run Clément through.

Henry's last order was for Henry de Navarre to follow him as Henry IV, the year 1589. During the French Revolution Henry III's grave was opened and his remains lost forever.

Henry's sister Margot and Margot's husband Henry de Navarre led separate lives, each taking numerous lovers. In fact, nearly all of Henry III's boys shared her bed at one time or another, to such an extent that Henry de Navarre called her Messalina and imprisoned her for 18 years (!) for her indiscretions, one of which, supposedly, was a plot to overthrow Henry of Navarre himself. During that time she wrote her memoirs, a tell-all concerning Henry III, published in 1628, thirteen years after her death, a book that caused a scandal. When they finally divorced she became, incredibly, friends with both her former husband and his new wife, Marie de' Medici, caring for their children, becoming a patron of the arts and a protectress of the poor. She died at age 61, having become fat and nearly bald, a woman who used life and allowed life to use her, never fleeing the storm, never seeking an illusive shelter that exists, in the end, for none of us. (3)

## HENRY IV

Henry IV was a direct descendant of Louis IX as well as being Henry III's cousin and the husband of Henry III's sister Margot. He was baptized in Pau in the Béarn manner: the holy water mixed with wine and garlic. Having changed religions six times, he did his best to uphold tolerance between Catholics and Protestants, all duly signed by Henry IV in the Edict of Nantes in 1598. This earned him the title of *le bon roi Henri*, Henry the Good. As Protestants were nonetheless heretics in the eyes of most Catholics, Henry escaped several attempts on his life, until stabbed by a dagger in a Parisian alley, rue de la Ferronnerie, the work of the religious fanatic François Ravaillac.

Henry IV attacked by Ravaillac.

The king had left the Louvre by carriage with the intention of visiting his first minister Sully, ill. Several of his favorites accompanied him in the carriage, of which Épernon was part. Other gentlemen were riding alongside on horseback, as well as valets on foot, most of which thought it more adventurous to take a shortcut through the nearby Saints-Innocents cemetery. The narrow street was full of onlookers and a few valets went on ahead to clear the passage of a cart of hay and another laden with wine barrels, signaling to the carriage driver that the passage was open. The king's carriage was at the level of an inn showing a heart pierced with an arrow when a man suddenly darted out from among those staring at Henry, his hair red, his beard brown, a knife already in hand that, leaning through the open carriage window, he plunged into Henry, a first blow just under his armpit, a second a little lower into the lung, cutting through the aorta, and a third lost in the robes of one of the passengers who tried to strike the assassin with his sword but was held back by Épernon who realized in a flash the necessity of the man's being interrogated later on. Then took place a strange, never explained incident. Several other men nearby, from six to eight, yelled out that the assassin had to die. When they were blocked from doing so, they disappeared into the crowds forming around the carriage, leaving the impression they had been trying to silence him.

Henry was taken to the Louvre, dead, where his wife Marie was informed. A woman devoted to astrology and soothsayers, she had warned Henry that one had predicted his death that day, and she had begged him to remain. Épernon was the first to kneel before Louis and Marie, the new king and regent. Louis, age 9, cried out that had he been there he would have killed the man with his sword.

François Ravaillac was a child of that part of the French population, the vast majority, outside of the court circle, who suffered from wars, famines and revolts, when not decimated by plagues, diseases and famines. Abandoned as a child by his father, thrown into jail for debt, he lived with his mother and found his only consolation in God. He tried to enter the orders but was immediately recognized as mentally unstable by the priests he approached, and a kind Jesuit told him to return home and spend the rest of his life in comforting prayer. He had come to Paris several times, always on foot, stealing food. Other men and bands of men were on the road, stealing, murdering, raping girls and young shepherds alone and isolated. Because there was no hope for them, they left no hope for others, finding a kind of inner peace by slitting the throats of the innocent, like Abraham and the sacrifice of his son Isaac.

Ravaillac's thumbs were crushed, his torture taking place on the very day of his crime, but never did he involve another, other than God who didn't believe in Henry's conversion to Catholicism and wanted him dead. His body was torn open by hooks, the wounds filled with molten lead. His four members were attached to horses and, incredibly, it took nearly two hours before one of his legs was finally pulled from his body. Only then did he die, his remains burned and the ashes dispersed.

Henry IV's heritage to France was that he brought order to Henry III's financial disorder, drained swamps, created forests, lined roads with trees, built canals and bridges, one of which is today's famous Pont Neuf. Tired of seeing artists going off to Italy to further their artistic education, he and his minister, the Duke of Sully, opened part of the Louvre to them and financed their art *à la Medici.* Education in general throughout France became a priority. They brought peace between France and Spain, and France and the Turks.

**Henry IV and Ravaillac**

It was Henry IV the originator of the American slogan ''a chicken in every pot'' when Henry decided to come to the aid of the average Frenchman, inaugurating a period of financial growth [*Si Dieu me prête vie, je ferai qu'il n'y aura point de laboureur en mon royaume qui n'ait les moyens d'avoir le dimanche une poule dans son pot!*] (14).

As noted, he liked boys but was especially known for his mistresses, earning him the nickname Henry the Gallant, *Henri le vert gallant* [*vert* meaning vigorous/spry/horny in old French].

Just after his assassination a statue was raised to him at the Pont Neuf, in 1614. Destroyed during the Revolution, but so beloved was Henry that it was reconstructed in 1818.


## LOUIS XIII


Louis XIII's mother Marie gave birth at Fontainebleau, in front of the court as she was obliged to do so that all could observe both the provenance of the child and its sex. His father, Henry IV, was the first to look at the boy's manhood and declared, ''It's as big as a big pea!'', while at his side Marie asked in her native Tuscan, ''*E machio? E machio*?'' The midwife didn't like the boy surrounded by so many people and Henry had to calm her by saying, Don't get angry, he belongs to everyone. Marie would later give him Elizabeth, destined for King Philip IV of Spain; Gaston, one son too many in that he would be a thorn in everyone's side until his death; and Henriette, Charles I's wife, Charles who would be beheaded by his own people.

**Louis by Jacopsen**

At age 4 Louis made the court laugh by playing with his boyhood [as reported by Héroard, Louis' private physician] and by simulating intercourse, all of which brought peals of laughter. Marie caressed her boy's member in front of everyone, and all the girls in the court were allowed to do the same, in public. But he wouldn't kiss a girl, and any who tried to kiss him got slapped. When Henry returned from the hunt Louis, who called him his ''*bon papa*'', was jubilant, throwing himself at his neck, covering him with the kisses he denied his female playmates.

Louis' word was already absolute. He expected to be immediately obeyed by his brothers Gaston, César and Alexandre, and Elizabeth, and by his playmates. At the slightest hesitation on their parts he would cry out that it was he the master, and he would have their heads. All of the children around him, and especially his brothers, would thoroughly hate him all their lives through. When he didn't get his way, Héroard wrote, he would kick, scream, throw whatever was at hand, crying out, I'll kill everyone! I'll kill God!

To break him, Henry IV recommended that he be thrashed with a veritable whip, whippings that began at age 2, Héroard wrote. ''I know from experience,'' said Henry, ''that this will do him good, as it did for me.'' But suddenly he would become uncontrollable, and refuse all obedience. He was supposed to un-hat himself before his father, as were all the king's subjects, and it infuriated Henry when the boy refused to do so. He would grab the hat from Louis' head, bringing forth terrible screams from the lad that not even whippings from birch branches could bring to an end. After Henry's death Louis' mother continued the beatings, after first offering him rewards if he would calm down, which he rarely did.

Louis desired nothing more than to run into his father's rooms in the early morning, never tiring of contemplating him nude, and from reports from the times, there was matter to contemplate. The boy's whole world was his father and nothing thrilled both more than Louis' being led by the hand of Henry through the gardens of Saint-Germain while Henry discussed politics with his councilors, never neglecting to look down and smile at the boy. At age three Henry dressed him in boots and spurs, sending Louis into throes of ecstasy. The court found it amusing to tell the boy that his father had arrived for a visit, laughing at both his excitement as he ran to greet him, and his cruel disappointment when he found that Henry wasn't there. From Henry, Louis learned to love the hunt, although he added to his passion a passion greater still for falcons and for his pet dogs, whose names and stalking skills he knew by heart. He had a huge collection of toy soldiers and drums, harquebusiers and toy cannons.

After Henry's death Louis' sobbing went on for days.

**Louis and mother Marie by Charles Martin.**

Following a period of mourning, Marie decided the court would become Florentine in nature, refined, brilliant, elegant and perfumed. In reality it was a remake of the court of Henry III, and with it came the mores of Henry III and Florence, debauch, mistresses and boys. Marie was Florentine as were the ancestors of one of te members of the court, Charles d'Albert de Luynes. At age 14 Luynes had been presented to Henry IV by his father, one of Henry IV's captains. After the death of Henry IV Luynes clearly saw that the route to future success passed through the bellies of noble wives, because historians insist on his being heterosexual, although he had perhaps been streetwise enough to envision the possibility of satisfying the needs of noblemen. Florentine sexual freedom was accompanied by Florentine ways, which were the ways of the most celebrated Florentine, Machiavelli--one kissed one's adversary in order to better stab him from behind.

Luynes

Louis had a passion for birds in general and falcons in particular, and it was Luynes the royal falconer. Louis had a passion for the hunt too, as said, perhaps even more than his passion for men. He was 10, Luynes was 33, as said, and it was love at first sight--for the boy, at least, but as Louis was the alpha and omega of French power and wealth, as he was now king, he became Luynes' ticket to the good life. For Louis a clarity had appeared, a man, calm and assuring, frank because he had little talent for dissimulation, and a ravaging smile that warmed the lad's cold heart, a heart dying for lack of attention. And then, sex was so simple between males, especially with a man who showed a boy the way, their bodies identical, their needs interchangeable and, afterwards, conversation so easy.

Louis' sexual interests had taken form while very young, and by age 9 he was sexually discovering himself with boys his age, notably in the palace parks. Héroard related that he adored watching couples during intercourse and would even be present, later, at the taking of his sister's and his half-sister's virginities during their wedding nights. Héroard kept a complete diary of the boy's coming of age, down to his orgasms. Héroard reported Louis' infatuation with his well-named coachman Saint-Amour, and several instances when Louis had sex with an army corporal, Escluseaux, when the boy was 15, which meant that he was not limiting his experiences to Luynes only. Escluseaux was called Pierrot and gave Louis sparrows to play with. When Louis saw him he threw his arms around his neck and covered him with kisses as he had his father. Louis was also attached to his half-brother Alexandre, a boy known as being wishy-washy, an attachment so intimate that it worried Marie who wondered what the court would say. Servants, farm hands, lackeys, stable lads and boys in charge of his dog kennels, were favorite pastimes when he was not with adults. Baradas, age 17, was of extreme importance during the six months they were together. He had been a groom in the stables called the *Petite Ecurie*. But one day Louis fell from a horse Baradas had given him and his hat tumbled off. Before he could pick it up the horse urinated on it, and from then on Baradas lost favor in his eyes. From then on, Luynes would be the uncontested love of his life. Héroard said that in his sleep Louis would say how much he loved Luynes and how handsome he was : *Le roi, dans son rêve a dit : "Qu'il est beau, qu'il est beau mon Luynes, que je l'aime."*

Louis ruled over a land delineated by rivers, the Rhone, the Meuse, the Saone and the Somme, containing around 15 millions souls, compared to 13 million in Italy, 12 in Russia, 9 in Spain and only 5 in England. Families then had an average of 8 children, half of which survived. Illegitimacies, the rule among the nobles, were nearly unknown among the people. A peasant lived 25 years, a noble a minimum of twice that. Priests taught how to read and write, as well as catechism, which left no space at all for free thought. A peasant's first occupation was survival. Most peasants learned of the death of a pope years afterwards, many had no idea of the year in which they labored, some ignored the century and even what the word century meant.

Louis by Frans Pourbus.

When Louis took Anne of Austria for wife both were 14, born nearly on the same day. The marriage night was often witnessed by others, which was necessary to ensure penetration. But as youths married early, and as puberty came much later then, a boy was at times unable or unwilling to penetrate the girl, simply because he hadn't enough testosterone to fuel his lust. Louis was placed on a bed with Anne, in front of his mother and others, but fell asleep. Later he told his physician Héroard that he had had her. Héroard asked to see his member, which was red [*Il y parassait la glande rouge*]. Héroard asked the boy if it was red due to entry or red due to rubbing against Anne. The boy's embarrassed replies left Héroard with the opinion that penetration had not taken place. This impression was reinforced afterwards when Héroard saw that there was no tender interaction between the pair, no embarrassed looks, no signs of complicity as one would see in lovers discovering love for the first time.

His mother Marie didn't care. She had it announced that her son had done his duty, and issued a simple proclamation: ''The king and queen, married by the church, consumed said marriage the night following their saintly wedding.'' After such humiliation the lad certainly threw himself into the welcoming arms and welcoming warmth of the ever-smiling Luynes.

Louis by Rubens

There was no doubt as to Louis' virility, as he would produce two sons and even as a child his lust pushed him to search out boys his age, as boys, always in search of discovery, have done since the world began. And if one is an ancient Greek in the soul, or a modern member of those parts of the world that celebrate gay marriage today, we know that there was nothing disquieting in his search for affection and consolation in those of his own sex. Louis installed Luynes in the Louvre in a room above his own, connected by a secret passage [a similar passage was recently found in one of James I's palaces between his rooms and those of George Villiers]. Meals were brought to both by servants, and Héroard noted that often Louis returned to his rooms at four in the morning. The fact that he felt obliged to return at all in order to escape scandal must have been an added incitement and stimulant, making his liaison with Luynes a breathless adventure. *''Le roi avait l'habitude de se relever pour aller dans le lit de M. de Luynes où ils s'amusaient, sans dormir jusqu'à quatre heures du matin.''*

In 1617 Luynes was 40 but still slim, his eyes caressing, his manners impeccable, his courtesy also. He had a handsome mustache and perfectly sculpted pointed goatee, and clear, frank, welcoming eyes masked whatever self-interest he may have harbored. He had bought his post as chief falconer, just as every court position had to be paid for, in cash, in the hope of turning it into a veritable fortune thanks to one's proximity to the absolute power of the king. Beyond sex, Luynes' influence on the king was decidedly soothing. His nature was Apollonian in his natural tendency towards the Golden Mean. There was nothing in excess with Luynes. Calm resolution of problems, a comforting presence at Louis' side, and advice that always tended to mediation, not confrontation, were Luynes' contributions.

It was Luynes who reigned, but this was perfect as Luynes sought exclusively the shadows, counseling Louis during their tête-à-têtes, giving him pep talks, bucking him up, stern when needed, but always loving, loving in the way of a heterosexual with a boy who worshipped him: there for the boy when needed, familiar only in moments of intimacy. The boy needed the physical comfort, but he needed the physical presence and the man's steady head far more. Louis made mistakes that were evident to those attending Louis' council meetings, but the boy had chosen his father Henry IV's advisors, all of which had witnessed his birth and had loved his father and now loved him, meaning that even Louis' worst gaffs created hardly a stir. He was just 16, for God's sake, said the men among themselves, what other 16-year-olds in the world could do better? Louis reported back to Luynes and together they plotted the future while living the present. Crises would come, but for the moment there was welcome calm before the storms, a badly needed timeout. Politically, the boy had lost his virginity. The other, heterosexually, would soon follow.

To maintain his place, Luynes rid the court of possible rivals. One was a captain of the Royal Guards, de la Curée, who visibly pleased Louis. He obliged de la Curée to leave, after which he gave his position to his brother Brantes. Another lad was Montpouillan who also clearly tempted the king. As he was a Huguenot, Luynes got his confessor, Arnoux, who was also, conveniently, Louis' confessor, to tell Louis that his place in the hereafter would be jeopardized should the heretic remain a part of his inner circle. Louis ordered him away, and when the lad came to take his leave, both broke down in sobs.

Now came to pass one of the strangest incidents in history. Perhaps one day a new Kinsey Report will surface in which we learn the current percentage of homosexuals, heterosexuals and bisexuals in America. I suspect that bisexuality is rising sharply (16), and if we can judge from thousands of years of Greek (24), Roman (25) and Renaissance history (9), it is more or less the norm, the norm in that during these three periods men were bisexual, passing from one sex to another in stressless fashion. Boys who are 100% heterosexual or 100% homosexual are perhaps, *perhaps*, becoming a rarity. Louis finally confessed to his confessor, Arnoux, that he had found the body of his wife Anne repugnant. Many others before and after Louis had tried heterosexual intercourse and had failed. Nijinsky fell into a depression when he married, Tchaikovsky turned to suicide. And the opposite is true, although so rare that we have to go back to the Greek boy who appealed to Zeus to allow him to feel as much passion for his male friends as they felt for each other. The last thing in the world he wanted was to be different from them. But because his friends continued to have no sexual interest for the boy, he killed himself.

This is the background of what played itself out in 1618 when Anne remained barren, word spreading from embassy to embassy that it was because the king refused to sleep with her. Once Arnoux had Louis' confession, he turned to Luynes and, conceivably without breaking his vows of confessional secrecy, made him aware of the situation--if, naturally, Luynes wasn't already aware, which, given the rapport between the lovers, seems unlikely. At the same time, Arnoux reportedly sent word of his discovery to the pope in Rome, who informed Madrid, since Anne of Austria's father was Philip of Spain. That European embassies were informed of Louis' weakness is certain. What follows may be certain too, except for the fact that most comes from modern, 20th century authors, all of whom were phagocytizing each other, not the most reliable way of learning the truth.

In any event, after Arnoux' visit to Luynes, Luynes told his wife--Marie de Rohan, age 17---to make herself available to the king. She did but the king wouldn't. Then the Spanish ambassador Monteleone told the maidens under the orders of Louis' wife to entice the king during one of his protocol visits to the queen, denuding themselves if necessary, as an encouragement to his performance. Louis was furious. He insulted them in the most vulgar terms and the girls reported back to Spain that sexually the king was worthless. It was said that Henry III's mother, Catherine de' Medici, had had female servants strip naked when serving her son during a banquet, the result of which were yawns and scowls at his mother's repeated attempts to make the young Henry ''operative''.

Communiqués at the time between embassies were masterpieces of restraint: the king ''lacked resolve'' said one, ''shows more modesty than temperament,'' said another.

The king had spied on couples engaged in intercourse since his earliest years. A voyeur at heart, he decided to renew the experience, perhaps as a prelude to his own *passage à l'acte*. He encouraged the marriage of a boy he appreciated, the Duke of Elbeuf, with Mlle de Vendôme. Héroard wrote in his diary that the king visited the couple that afternoon and remained with them for three hours. The Venetian ambassador Angelo Contarini wrote to the Serenissima that Louis had been present during the consummation, one that Elbeuf accomplished two times in front of the king who had been enchanted by the sight. Supposedly the bride had turned to Louis and told him, according to Contarini, ''to do the same thing with his queen.'' Says Héroard: *"Suivez mon exemple, Sire, et faites la même chose avec la reine."*

Louis' wife Anne of Austria.

Instead, he went to find Luynes! Every night that followed was spent between Louis and Luynes, with the king, according to Héroard, always returning, before sunrise, to his own bed. Luynes, who was steadily enjoying *his* wife, was reported to have been exasperated that Louis was incapable of doing the same with his *own* wife. That said, as his entire fortune and position at the court depended on the king's will, Luynes must have felt, at the same time, very reassured that his own place in Louis' heart was secure.

Finally, writes Héroard, Luynes took Louis to his wife's rooms. He had Anne strip naked and despite Louis' strenuous objections, Luynes denuded the king and, taking him in his arms, forced him into Anne's bed. The biographer of the American actor Tyrone Power said that homosexual Tyrone, who was married, could penetrate his wife only during orgies, while surrounded by naked boys whose beautiful asses and vagina-encircled dicks plunged to ecstatic release (19). Perhaps Luynes aided Louis in similar fashion, caressing the body he so intimately knew. Perhaps.

The next morning there were two humorous surprises. Héroard served the king a tisane, as if he had gotten over a severe illness, and Luynes was roundly congratulated by the whole court, as if it had been *he* the valiant taker of virginities. Word spread to the embassies that the deed had been done, *three years* after the wedding night. Bisexuals and heterosexuals reading this will wonder how Louis could have hesitated so long. Homosexuals will wonder how he was able to get an erection, unless Luynes' encouragements had indeed been persuasive. That said, it turned out that Louis may not at all have been as homosexual as even he thought, because following his performance he honored Anne on other occasions, producing at least one still-born child and one lost through a miscarriage, before the birth of the future Louis XIV [heterosexual] and Louis XIV's younger brother [an insatiable homosexual]. According to Héroard, Louis' visits to Luynes gradually fell off until Luynes' death, while those to his wife increased, without Luynes' intervention.

During this time the exceedingly intelligent Cardinal Richelieu had entered the court thanks to Louis' mother, Richelieu who gained influence over Louis and set his sights on personally destroying Luynes. But despite Richelieu's genius, a genius thanks to the grace of a perfect brain and years of study, he would always come up against the insurmountable wall of Louis' love for Luynes, a fact perhaps beyond Richelieu's powers of comprehension because it was centered around the heart. Richelieu's battle against Luynes was similar to that of Sisyphus, and like Sisyphus he was unaware that it was both useless and everlasting.

**Luynes**

Then, Luynes fell ill with scarlet fever. He was regularly visited by Louis, according to Héroard's journal, until the fear of contagion forced Louis to flee. From then on the king refused to touch Luynes' letters when Luynes, knowing he was going to die, wrote to beg him to look after his family. It is written that one man was left to care for Luynes, to see his body placed in a casket and expedited to his family estate. There are no details except that at rest halts the soldiers played cards on the coffin.

Louis was said to have uttered: ''I loved this man because he loved me, but something in him was lacking.'' He went on to say that he had had it with favored followers, and that from then on he would rule alone, a decision his mother applauded when she heard it.

Louis and Luynes' love was certainly not that known to Achilles and Patroclus, Alexander and Hephaestion, but it had saved a boy from the terrors of facing abandonment and solitude, and the falconer had risen to heights known only to the majestic birds he cherished. Luynes was definitely a man, with a man's quirks, but a man. What the boy, just turned 20, would become we will now discover.


Richelieu's entry into the king's council was like a wolf in the henhouse, the chickens in the council didn't stand a chance. Richelieu's reign was immensely aided by the startling decline of Spain. How a country of vast wealth, built on the unequaled courage and perseverance and *insane* ambition of the likes of Cortés and Pizarro, could fall so low so fast is a true warning to the frailty of existence. The rise of England, under men of equally wondrous ability such as Drake, would succeed in lands as far west as America and as far south as Australia and New Zealand, plus the subcontinent of India. The English didn't even leave the diminishing supplies of silver and gold to Spain, but took what they wanted with their war ships, down to stealing the Spanish ships themselves. And Louis got on the English bandwagon by marrying his sister Henriette to the English king Charles I. In the Netherlands the Protestants were bleeding Spain white, as nothing was ever more expensive in time, men and material than maintaining an army. At the same time, the Holy Roman Empire under Ferdinand was facing disunity, a worldwide perfect storm waiting to be dealt with by a man such as Richelieu.

It was with this in mind that Louis summoned Richelieu to Versailles, soon to be converted into today's wonder by Louis' son the future Louis XIV. For hours and hours the two men, facing a huge chimney fire in Louis' personal retreat, one as simple as a manor house, discussed how they would, together, put France on the track to preeminence, a discussion that sealed their destinies and the destiny of one of the world's finest achievements, France itself.

France would become Europe's first power. The nobles would be disciplined and forced into complete obedience, but not destroyed as Richelieu wished access to the nobility for himself and his family. All unnecessary fortifications owned by the nobles, unnecessary for the defense of France, would be torn down. Lords in disagreement would be hanged, as soon 133 would be in the province of the Poitou, alone. Heretics would be put up with but crushed if they revolted against the crown--the freedom of conscience had its limits! Catholicism would remain the nation's official religion. Culture would not be forgotten, and indeed Richelieu put down the foundation for the Académie française which would govern the use and evolution of the French language, the reason why I have a bedside dictionary of English words, my first language, but do not need one for French, the reason I can read Molière without the slightest difficulty, but need said dictionary for Shakespeare. New ports would be built, as well as a fleet of ships. France would also expand New France, New France founded by Jacques Cartier's exploration in 1534 and covered over 1/3$^{rd}$ of today's America, from Canada to Mexico [a territory surrendered to Spain and England in 1763 but a huge portion (1/4$^{th}$ of the present United States), called Louisiana, was returned to France in 1800, only to be sold by Napoleon in 1803].


Richelieu had been aided in his rise to power by Antoine Coiffier-Ruzé, Marquis d'Effiat, whose chateau Richelieu considered his second home. It was said he used an adjoining building as a torture chamber where there was a chair that could be tipped backwards, like that used in Burton's *Sweeney Todd*, the fall into an oubliette ending the lives of his enemies.

Richelieu wanted to know what the sphinxlike king was thinking, so he came up with a plan to place Antoine's son Cinq-Mars in Louis' bed, the first step towards which was to make the boy commander, at age 15, over a company of guards.

Cinq-Mars

When Cinq-Mars joined the court, he found what the French call a *panier de crabes*, everyone crawling over everyone else for standing, for advancement, for gains of every nature, like crabs, the least of which was sex, because sex was so easy and ubiquitous. Keeping a girl virgin to ensure a good marriage, *that* was the challenge, the reason lips were true second sexes. When a court lad eventually became satiated in court pleasure, so blasé he was reduced to spending his time playing cards, there were other sites, like the Marais and its libertines who reveled in composing poems, discussing philosophy and debauching themselves in orgies to the extent that even these became boring. Luckily there was always a war somewhere, or duels, or street brawls.

After Luynes' death Louis had promised to dedicate himself wholly to his kingdom, just as Elizabeth had become the Virgin Queen, England itself her husband. But his inner emptiness needed someone, someone who was certainly not Richelieu whom he may have really detested as most writers claim. Richelieu was aware of the void, as vast as the emptiness of space, and knew just the lad to fill it. Richelieu introduced him to Cinq-Mars and suggested that Louis name him his Grand Master of the Wardrobe. Most historians say Cinq-Mars knew that the job, the most intimate of those involving the king, was pure slavery, opening him up to both verbal and physical abuse, because the king regularly hit the help when in a nasty mood. In addition, the king's mores were not only known by the court boys, all the boys, but snickered at, if not openly guffawed, by those who even shared them, and it was largely *that* the reason why Cinq-Mars at first refused. And anyway, even boys who preferred boys would have no sexual attraction for the pasty, physically unpleasing monarch, a sufferer of headaches and diarrhea.

Richelieu went to Cinq-Mars's mother, whose ambition encouraged her to put her full weight on her son to accept, as did Cinq-Mars's friends, well aware of the wealth and power that would be his. And so on the lad's 18th birthday, the 27th of March, 1638, Cinq-Mars was named Grand Master of the Wardrobe, thanks to which he would lose his beautiful head four years later, at age 22.

Cinq-Mars's mother was wealthy but stingy, and Cinq-Mars had never been able to dress in a way that would flatter his looks. Now the kingdom's tailors were literally at his feet, certain their creations, worn by Cinq-Mars, would inspire the king himself. He had 300 pairs of boots, 52 outfits, cloaks, hats, wigs and accessories. His breeches were lined with white satin, each garment edged in gold and silver, with cascades of lace, Philippe Erlanger tells us in his book *The King's Minion*. As Cinq-Mars had imagined, the king was rough, but one wonders if it were not a way of playing with the boy, as one who doesn't want to appear too easy. Louis had admitted to his former lover Saint-Simon that in affairs of the heart his life was not the simplest, because he knew, thanks to his position, that he could have whomever he wanted and, he continued to confess to Saint-Simon, ''I must nonetheless not forget that while I am king and they must obey, I must also remember that God forbids this.'' At the same time, Louis continued, he was subject to his lusts. Erlanger gives a description of Louis that I find apt: ''He was timid but given to terrible fits of violence. He was an oversensitive, suspicious, jealous despot who practically abdicated to his Minister

[Richelieu]. He was indecisive but stubborn, a rigid moralist with a taste for puerile pleasures, a wounded soul given to passing stringent judgment on others, a compound of anguish and conviction, pride and self-effacement, dynamism and submissiveness.''

Richelieu – Louis - Cinq-Mars by Claudius Jacquand.

As for Cinq-Mars, he was a breath of fresh air, all light and charm, always happy, able to give himself pleasure whenever he wished because not only were the girls at court available, they vied with one another for the ardor concealed in his satin breeches, and Cinq-Mars never hesitated when cornering a maiden to grasp her hand and place it on the rigid manhood under the tissue, searching her eyes for consent. His exploits were on all lips and there were certainly boys as jealous as girls, but other than Louis himself, whom he could not avoid due to his power and inexhaustible source of wealth, there was not a hint of his frequenting other lads. One of Cinq-Mars's girls, Marion de Lorme, was said to have been a dazzling beauty, wrote La Rochefoucauld, adding that her intellect was no less pleasurable. In time she would become an experienced courtesan, perhaps thinking back to Cinq-Mars as women of a similar time would remember Barry Lyndon. In any case, he spent his nights with Marian and saw her four times a day, each time in a new set of clothes, perhaps ''honoring'' her at each visit. His mother was said to have been apoplectic, but he ignored her.

The Incident of the Peas sealed Cinq-Mars's triumph at court. Louis and his army took Hesdin in 1639, which had been captured by the Holy Roman Emperor Charles V in 1553. From there he went to Mézières where he was welcomed by the Duke of Nemours, a young, handsome lad who instantly became aware of Louis' weakness for the boy accompanying him. As Nemours was a noble and Cinq-Mars only a gentleman, Nemours decided to rib him mercilessly in front of the court, to put him in his place, something easy to do as a gentleman was not allowed to retaliate to a noble's aggression. But Cinq-Mars, motored by adolescent testosterone, had no intention of being intimidated. At a meal the young Nemours spit a pea in the lad's direction, and Cinq-Mars answered back by spitting one into Nemours' eye. A scuffle ensued, both boys separated by their attendants. Louis got word of the affair and no one doubted that Cinq-Mars was in trouble. But Louis made a public show of affection to Cinq-Mars, placing a hand on his shoulder, shocking the court down to their boots because, first, Louis hadn't taken Nemours' side as tradition demanded and, second, he had never ever shown such public favor for one of his lads or men, not even for Luynes.

When Richelieu found out, he was in heaven, as it was he who had placed Cinq-Mars in Louis' bed, and now he would reap the rewards by having the boy work for him, undercover. Soon Louis was sending his personal carriage for Cinq-Mars's displacements. That Cinq-Mars was seeing girls throughout the day, that he rode off at night to be with a certain maiden, leaving the moment Louis went to bed and returning just before his awakening--catching snatches of sleep whenever possible--meant nothing because Louis knew nothing of the lad's highly furnished sexual escapades.

The boy wanted balls and festivities and Louis even participated at one such extravaganza, but he was a puritan at heart, always in quest of seducing God while seducing boys, boring Cinq-Mars to tears by what the French call his *préchi-précha* ways--his sermonizing and moralizing. He wanted the boy constantly at his side, especially when he visited his dog kennels and aviaries, and during the hunt, while the boy dreamed of being naked with a naked girl. Cinq-Mars rode off nightly to be with Marion, presumably convincing her to attend orgies in the Marais, before riding back to Saint-Germain and the king's awakening, the resulting fatigue said to have drained part of his beauty from his face.

When Richelieu's attempts to make Cinq-Mars his personal spy failed, Richelieu did the following, brought to us by Erlanger: ''He told him how and why a dandy who had no greater claims to fame than a pretty face had been made to rise to the summit of favor, why he had been chosen and practically forced on the king. Henry d'Effiat was a total nonentity, an insignificant nothing. The only existence he had was that of a servile instrument created in the interests of the cardinal.''

Cinq-Mars, sobbing, left Richelieu, decided to seal Richelieu's fate, but as an inexperienced lad of only 20, he would seal only his own.

On their shared pillow, Louis let Cinq-Mars known that he was growing tired of Richelieu, and Cinq-Mars let him know that the only way he would ever be uncontested king was with Richelieu dead. On the other hand, Louis allegedly told the boy that if ever he had to choose between the two, his favor would always go to Richelieu. The boy was warned, but what boy ever heeds advice contrary to his generous opinion of himself?

The man who would see Cinq-Mars to an early grave was the king's own brother Gaston, an arrogant, brainless poof who had continually revolted against Louis, and sought Louis' death, had begged his forgiveness on his knees, multiple times, and would soon sacrifice Cinq-Mars by turning traitor.

Things came to a head when Cinq-Mars met with Gaston at the Hôtel de Venice, a hôtel being a whole building owned by one person, in this case Gaston's squire, where Gaston stabled his horses [the post of squire had cost the lad a fortune, but now he owned his own building in the heart of Paris, the Marais].

Cinq-Mars told Gaston that Louis had had enough of Richelieu and wanted to free himself so he, Louis, could finally reign unhampered. Gaston promised he would support Cinq-Mars to the bitter end, and agreed that the destruction of Richelieu had become essential. Gaston then went to see the queen, Anne, who hated Richelieu and needed Gaston to assure her reign as regent at the time of Louis' death, Louis who was always in more or less bad health. She knew she was smarter than Gaston and so did not hesitate to encourage him. Louis had made it clear to Cinq-Mars on numerous occasions that he and the people were tired of Richelieu, the people because they witnessed the luxury of his carriage, his gorgeously attired musketeers, his palace that was perhaps not equal in grandeur to the Louvre but was in any case infinitely more extended, the people who hurt under his taxes and died due to his wars, fighting them or victims to them. Time and again Louis had accused Richelieu for being the true king, leaving him, Louis, in the shadows. He blamed Richelieu for the conflicts on every French border. Naturally, Richelieu had done nothing without the full consent of Louis. One wonders to what point Cinq-Mars blamed the old head on his pillow for not taking matters in hand, since a single order from Louis would put anyone in the kingdom at the mercy of the executioner, as Cinq-Mars himself would learn.

With the proof in hand, Richelieu arranged a meeting with the king at Richelieu's quarters. Two beds were placed side by side as at Versailles, in front of the immense fireplace, and both men spent hours in fraternal conversation

Cinq-Mars was arrested. Gaston again begged for forgiveness. He promised Louis he would retire to his lands and never interfere again in the king's governance, and that he would never again raise troops. Richelieu told Louis' wife Anne that she could sleep tranquilly, as he believed that Louis would soon be dead and knew that Anne would be named regent until the 13th birthday of Louis XIV. Richelieu himself met with Cinq-Mars who denied ever planning Richelieu's death. Were it not for Gaston who confessed Cinq-Mars's role, the lad might have saved his head.

Pierre Séguier, councilor of France and chief prosecutor, personally visited Cinq-Mars. Perhaps honestly, perhaps genuinely, Séguier promised the lad that the king, who still loved him, would spare his life, and that the boy would face only a short imprisonment if he gave a complete confession. This Cinq-Mars gave, while denying his intention of wanting Richelieu dead.

That Louis was the unluckiest prince who ever lived doesn't excuse his dismissal of Luynes with, ''I loved him because he loved me.'' And how can one spend years with a lad, share his bed with the boy he was devoted to, in the most intimate embrace known to man, and end it all by taking the lad's life? A golden imprisonment could have been envisioned, but not the taking of one's unique existence.

Cinq-Mars never asked for Louis' grace. The execution took place in a public square, the platform seven feet above a huge crowd come to see the king's favorite put to death, the windows of the surrounding buildings rented out in exchange for coins of pure gold, the roofs overhung by masses as clinging as barnacles. Father Malavalette accompanied Cinq-Mars. The boy held himself straight and proud, saying only that he was in a hurry to know immortal life. At the block the priest undressed the neck and cut the lad's locks. ''My God, what a world!'', were the boy's final words before the axe fell, taking his precious life.

Cinq-Mars in the forefront.

The death of Cinq-Mars was not enough for Richelieu. He deprived Cinq-Mars's brother and sister of their lands and heritage and ordered Cinq-Mars's chateau reduced to rubble and the neighboring woods cut down. He neglected only to sow the earth with salt.

Richelieu and Louis met back in Fontainebleau. Richelieu had to be held up by servants so he could greet the king properly. He congratulated him on having recovered his senses by ridding himself of his infatuation with Cinq-Mars. We don't know Louis' reply but it was said both men had tears in their eyes, so choked up were they in each other's presence. Two old, empty, dying men gladdened by a lad's death, one stinking from arm infections, the other from recurrent diarrhea; both in competition as to who hated the guts of the other more; both sealed in mutual need, like viruses that depended on a host's blood.

A week later Richelieu coughed up blood and had difficulty breathing. Louis visited his bedside and personally fed him two egg yolks. Shortly after he left, Richelieu breathed his last.

With death at his doorstep, Louis publicly asked pardon from all those he had harmed, placing the blame for his actions on years of Richelieu's tyranny. Gravely ill with abdominal pains and diarrhea, he hung on for three long months until the inevitable, at age 42. Moments before dying he asked for his son to be brought to him. ''What's your name, my son?'' ''Louis XIV, dear Papa.'' ''Not yet, but soon.'' Louis XIV's reign would be one of the longest in history, 72 years, far longer than that of Ramses II. The last word goes to a servant of Anne's who declared that, when all is considered, ''*Il ne s'aimait pas lui-même.*'' Louis didn't even love himself.

As I'm an unrepentant humanist I can only hope that, with a bit of luck, it was Luynes that Louis found at the Pearly Gates, Luynes who would again show him the way.

# <u>PART II</u>

## THE COURT OF LOUIS XIV

Sex was a primary occupation and distraction in the court of Louis XIV, the floors of corners, nooks and recesses cleaned of spilled semen in the early mornings, French gardens, usually geometric in form, were purposely designed with wooded and bushy areas for nightly assignations, along with caves and discrete niches behind waterfalls. Louis XIV's brother's wife, Elizabeth Charlotte of Bavaria, known as Princess Palatine [see Sources], claimed ''I have become so knowledgeable here in France'' on the subject of courtly sex ''that I could write books on it'', but she did even better, leaving behind 60,000 letters, in one of which she writes, concerning her husband, Louis XIV's brother, known as *Monsieur,* ''I do my best to persuade Monsieur that I do not want to disturb him in his entertainment and love of men'', adding even that she was proud of this special form of virility, historically shared by Heracles, Alexander the Great, Caesar and Theseus. What she didn't like was his spending *her* money and giving *her* jewels to what she called Monsieur's ''*divertissements*'' and his ''*Männerlieb*'' (44). Love between men was reserved for ''people of quality who discuss it openly'', the Italian vice beyond the understanding of uneducated common folk, ''accepted even by God'', Princess Palatine further stating that ''since the days of Sodom and Gomorrah our Lord has not punished anyone for this reason'', a sin that had existed ''only as long as the world was not peopled.'' She knew that in France it was punished death, but in reality death was restricted to the ''common folk'' she referred to.

It nonetheless took some imagination for her to compare her husband to masculine lovers of men like Alexander, Heracles and Theseus, her husband Philippe d'Orléans who was pot-bellied, farded and who ''wore shoes so high he seemed mounted on stilts,'' wrote Saint-Simon [see Sources], adorned like women ''powdered and covered in perfumes'', his preference cross-dressing that he had to limit because of his being ''imprisoned in the dignity and grandeur of princes, free to be himself only during masked balls and carnivals.''

As a youth Monsieur was renowned for his beauty, ''the prettiest child in the world'', stated a duchess, whose preference for men certainly stemmed from the boys surrounding his homosexual father Louis XIII and the use Louis' court made of them (37). The singularity came from how Monsieur's brother the future Louis XIV escaped the Italian vice, Louis who had known girls from his earliest puberty, one of whom, whose father was a palace gardener, caused an immense stir when she became pregnant, the court rejoicing in the proof that the future Louis

XIV could sire children, which put the gardener on the road to what was, for him, wealth, thanks to the funds accorded the future king's bastard. Girls throughout all history were sources of wealth to their fathers, provided they were placed in the right beds, the bloodstained sheets publicly exhibited the next morning the proof of their virginity. Girls destined for the nobility, and those meant for kings, had to remain virgin, an example Marie and Anne Boleyn--the first Henry VIII's mistress, the second his wife--who had grown up in the French courts of Louis XII and François I, where girls learned to use their mouths as second sexes, their bodies fully open to every form of arousal except the penetration that would rupture hymens, François I who was accompanied on hunting expeditions by his bed, the reputed size of his member the promise of pleasure for any lass he encountered during the hunt, a coin of gold welcomed by her father or husband.

**François I by Jean Clouet. His extensive nose, and what it symbolized, was greatly appreciated by demoiselles.**

Omnisexuality (16) was the rule, limiting oneself to one sex rather than another nonsensical, although there were preferences, at times so strong that one did restrict one's sexual exploration to just one sex. Of great importance was also the social context, one's inclination governed by where one could better butter one's bread, which encouraged fathers to replace themselves in the beds of the powerful with their sons.

Cardinal Richelieu had placed boys in the bedchamber of Louis XIII as spies, aware of the unrestrained pillow talk between Louis and his lovers. Cardinal Mazarin went infinity farther. Olympia Mancini was part of the extended Italian relations of Mazarin, six nieces and three nephews that Mazarin placed in the grandest beds in Europe, collectively known as the Mazarinettes, Mazarin's tactic for gaining influence and gleaning information that Mazarin had learned from Richelieu who had employed Cinq-Mars for the same purposes (39). He placed his nephew Philippe Jules Mancini, Duke of Nevers, in the sleeping quarters of Louis XIV's young brother Philippe d'Orléans, Mancini that some historians believe was Mazarin's own son, while reserving Olympia for Louis' pleasure, a girl that historians speculate may have been the boy's first amorous experience, although she was replaced by Olympia's sister, Marie, who pleased the future king even more, one who apparently used her talents to give him pleasure without endangering her virginity, the proof of which was the stained bedding when she was later married off to a noble. Mazarin believed that a homosexual prince would be a lesser threat to Louis during his reign, and because Philippe would hopefully have no children, having spent his semen between boy buttocks, there would be no threat to Louis' dynastic plans. It was nonetheless rumored that Louis himself had taken an ardent interest in one of Mazarin's nephews, perhaps Jules, perhaps another.

Louis knew he could have whomever he wanted, and even valets knew they would be rewarded by bringing candidates to his bedchamber, a procedure fully accepted by the queen, and even today in France an upper-class girl is told by her mother, before her marriage, to accept her husband's philandering, because that's the way it is [*C'est comme ça et pas autrement*], a confession made to me by one of my private Parisian students, well into her seventies, the wife of a former minister, who made it clear that she had a certain benevolence concerning me personally, as did another aged student who proposed putting me up in a Biarritz hotel adjoining that of her and her husband, proof that the philandering worked both ways (7). Primi Visconti [see Sources] wrote, ''Every woman was born with the ambition to become the King's favorite'', which was true. Yet Louis felt the need to honor those he found extraordinary with an official title, that of *maîtresse déclaré*, or royal mistress, a position soon quasi-institutionalized although it was never fully official, but it was visible, as royal mistresses cared not only for the sexual needs of the king, but also served the queen and the royal children. Madame de Montespan, a royal mistress of great power, personally prepared girls for Louis' pleasure, thusly fulfilling the role that had been Diane de Poitiers' in choosing and readying girls for a night with Henry II (3), while at least one mistress dismissed by Louis gained revenge by stating that Montespan spurned the physical ''act'' with Louis due to the smallness of Louis' scepter.

A good mistress filled her apartments with intoxicating flowers and provided the best wines. She became a student of Louis' moods and could read his every facial expression, her aim to soothe him after a day's ups-and-downs. Some never left their apartments for fear that Louis would appear and need food, conversation and sex. She could not show fatigue, illness, anger or boredom, and she did not allow herself to show an emotion that might upset the king. The reality of what went on sexually must certainly have been influenced by the fact that some didn't bathe for weeks and even inserted head scratchers into their coiffures to ease the irritation of flea and lice bites. Hair was not washed, it was powdered, a form of dry-cleaning.

Louis did manage to spend almost every night with his wife, reserving his dalliances with his courtesans for other moments, all the while leading the nation without the advice of a chief minister. His marriage to Maria Theresa had been lucky and fecund, six children of whom the oldest was known as the Grand Dauphin, born in 1661, dead at age 49, *dauphin* the title given to the eldest son of a king of France, stemming from lands--the Dauphiné--transmitted to a king's first-born male, often also called Monseigneur. A second son was born two years later, Philippe. The number of Louis' mistresses attested to his virility, just one of whom, the Marquise de Montespan, gave him seven children. Louis was more faithful to his second wife, Françoise d'Aubigné,

Marquise de Maintenon, most probably due to his advancing age. An anecdote has Louis' brother Philippe enter Louis' bedchamber, the bedcovers drawn back to show him naked with de Maintenon, Louis stating ''In the condition in which you see me with Madame de Maintenon, you can imagine what she is to me'' (38), which could be read in two ways, either he was erect, signaling his excitation for her, or not, signifying his lack of lust. That he could appear naked, erect or not, in front of Philippe, indicated a certain intimacy between brothers. As for Madame de Maintenon, she warned Louis that if he didn't put an end to the rampant homosexuality at court, God would punish him. ''Should I start with my own brother?'' asked Louis rhetorically.

Louis transformed a royal hunting lodge into today's Versailles where he moved the court in 1682, away from the revolts, intrigues and cabals in Paris, Versailles open, more easily defended, surrounded by walls of pikes, the byways lighted and patrolled by an army of police.

Louis set out to immortalize his reign by becoming the centralized source of all activity, a veritable Sun King, Versailles the world center of painting, sculpture, theater, dance and music, a standing army offering protection more dissuasive than that offered today's presidents and sultans. Saint-Simon wrote that ''there was nothing he liked so much as flattery, or, to put it more plainly, adulation; the coarser and clumsier it was, the more he relished it.'' Voltaire added that ''Louis' vanity was the cause for his bellicosity. It is certain that he passionately wanted glory, rather than the conquests themselves. In the acquisition of Alsace, half of Flanders and elsewhere, what he really liked was the name he made for himself'', Voltaire adding, in his *The Age of Louis XIV*, that ''Louis' reign was not only one of the four great ages in which reason and culture flourished, but the greatest ever.'' A position agreed to by Napoleon who described him as ''the only King of France worthy of the title.''

Women gained power in Louis' court because, wrote a courtier, ''graces'' were preferred to brute strength. Discretion, cunning and dissembling one's ambitions and passions replaced, at Versailles, the nobles' former reliance on swagger, arrogance, strength and violence. The transformation was easy because what counted at Versailles was simply being there, the center of power, where prestige came through a regard from Louis, ruin when, for one reason or another, he chose ''not to see'' someone he held in disfavor, while a moment of public conversation with the king assured a noble's popularity that day, and the sexual benevolence of those who imagined him close to Louis that night, which was also true of those chosen to hand him his stockings in the morning, or were allowed to be present as he used his *chaise percée*.

A *chaise percée* and that used by Madame de Pompadour on
the far right.

Louis and the queen sat in armchairs, others in chairs without arms if they were destined for his children and brother, while those of rank were given padded stools, the nobles obliged to stand. When Louis' brother Philippe d'Orléans said he wanted a chair with arms, Louis reminded him that part of the respect for the king came through ceremony, and that one day Philippe himself would perhaps replace Louis and be happy to continue the distinctions that empowered him over the others. ''The day that they regard us as their equals, all the prestige of our position will be destroyed.''

Strict rules of etiquette governed every activity, a necessity in controlling the vast number of people present at Versailles each day, from 3,000 to 10,000. The honor of being in the presence of the king, to stand out thanks to one's clothing, beauty and wit, made service to Louis the ultimate goal of each noble, a far cry from the court of Henry III where boys and Henry's little dogs could freely enter Henry's chambers without being announced (3). Positions in the court were bought, from valets to barbers to stable boys, who could serve as intermediaries between outsiders and those of importance within the court, paid in consequence, an example given in the chapter on Louis XIII where a meeting between Louis' brother Gaston and plotters against Richelieu took place in a townhouse in the Marais, bought by a boy who had paid to work in the king's stables, earning a fortune afterwards by introducing outsiders to nobles, while wealth of this kind was greatly multiplied for nobles who could get outsiders into a room where Louis XIV was merely present.

The members of court that counted the most were, of course, the king and his queen, followed by the first in line for the throne: the Dauphin, the king's other sons, then his daughters, the sons of the former king and the daughters of the former king. The major titles of nobility were, in order of importance: duc, comte, marquis, vicomte and baron, while ecclesiastical peers ranked ahead of lay peers, meaning that an ecclesiastical comte counted far more than a non-ecclesiastical comte. Originally ''comte'' referred to someone in charge of a county, a position that was not hereditary, ''marquis'' someone in charge of borderlands called *marshes* in old French, ''duc'' signifying a leader, and so on, all of which eventually became hereditary.

A monarch was originally a person who was the head of a state for life, today a symbolic role in England, one that was absolute in the time of Louis XIV. At the death of Charlemagne his empire was divided, his grandsons assuming control over West Francia, Italy and parts of Germany, West Francia becoming the nucleus of France. One of the earliest descendants of Charlemagne's sons was Hugh Capet, elected in 987, founder of the Capetians and their two offshoots, the houses of Valois and Bourbon, who ruled France until the French Revolution of 1789, Louis XIV a Bourbon.

Nobles were just under kings. They possessed land they distributed to men called vassals, feudal tenants, the basis of feudalism, on condition that the vassals give homage and provide military support, food and money. Vassals ruled the peasantry, uneducated laborers, often unfree, who did the planting of crops, the raising of animals and served as military fodder in times of war, their power greatly improved thanks to the black plague which killed off hundreds of thousands of laborers, thusly obliging the vassals to pay dearly for the services of the survivors, feudalism ending with the French Revolution. The nobles built their own fortifications, which could endanger the very existence of a king, as during the time of Henry II when his wife Eleanor and his sons revolted against him, based on the support of nobles and their fortifications (27). The church was of huge importance until it subverted itself through excesses like the selling of indulgences and the promise that a soul in hell would be immediately freed the moment a coin entered the alms bowl of a priest. This led to protestation from Luther and Calvin, the establishment of Protestantism, which increased the power of kings solicited by popes to protect what remained of papal authority, Louis XIV the first king to put an end to heresy in France. The people agreed to the growing powers of monarchs in exchange for protection, beginning with fear of the Vikings and continuing onto Agincourt where the armies of England's Henry V destroyed the cream of French nobility. Philippe le Bel and François I were the first great kings of France, followed by the greatest warrior of them all, a man clothed in red, Cardinal Richelieu, who, using King Louis XIII as his tool (37), set France on the course to Empire. He reduced the number of fortifications ruled by the nobles [destruction greatly increased by Louis XIV's minister Colbert], stabilized relations between Catholics and Protestants, opening the gates for Louis XIII's son Louis XIV and the first absolutist monarchy--known to the world as the *Roi-Soleil* and *l' État, c'est moi*--Louis who had the genial idea of welcoming the nobles to an unequaled palace--in fact their obligation to be present several months a year--a palace that offered entertainment by Molière, music by Lully, gardens by Le Nôtre with their monumental fountains and fireworks, food of unparalleled beauty and savor, and the thrilling possibility of entering one's sword into a different sheath each and every night. An invitation to Versailles and the honor of a moment in the presence of Louis had nobles groveling before the Kings of Kings.

Only the passage of time reduced the brilliance of this

exceptional man, 72 years of it spent on the throne, and although he is portrayed, up to the end, as healthy, and the possessor of strong and beautiful legs, he suffered from diabetes, gout, dizziness, headaches and dental abscesses, in such pain at the end that he ''yielded up his soul without effort, like a candle going out'' (33), at age 77, the average lifespan for nobles 40 years. His last words of advice to his heir were, ''Do not follow the bad example which I have set you; I have often undertaken war too lightly and have sustained it for vanity. Do not imitate me, but be a peaceful prince, and may you apply yourself to alleviate the burdens of your subjects.'' Louis was fully aware of his mortality, having told his first son, at the death of a court noble, ''What becomes of the grandeurs of the world, we shall come to that, you and I.'' Because his legitimate and legitimized sons perished before him, as well as his grandsons, Louis' heir became his five-year-old great-grandson Louis, Duke of Anjou, the future Louis XV. Louis XV was described as ''a perpetual adolescent called to do a man's job'' (35), a reign of ''debilitating stagnation'', a man ruled by his mistresses, the center of his interests boudoirs, bedrooms and debauch, the catalyst of the French Revolution and the beheading of his son.

**Louis XIV**

## MAZARIN'S MAZARINETTES

Philippe Jules Mancini, 1641-1707, was Cardinal Mazarin's nephew. Born in Italy, his mother took him to Paris following the death of his aristocratic father in order to benefit from his uncle Mazarin's all-powerful position as the major influence of Queen

Anne's regency of the future Louis XIV. Philippe entered the court along with his five sisters, all of whom would become immensely powerful in their own right, one married to the Duc de Vendôme; another, Marie, thought to have been Louis XIV's very-first real love; Hortense who became Charles II of England's mistress; and a Mancini cousin who married into the wealthy and well-established family of Alphonso IV d'Este (6), her daughter James II of England's wife.

Mazarin decided to use Philippe as his own personal tool the moment he saw the handsome lad, whom he set to work to seduce and deflower Louis XIV's brother Philippe d'Orléans, whom Mazarin wanted to unman by changing him into the court's prettiest cross-dresser, Mazarin who knew or assumed that Mancini was already familiar with what the court called the Italian vice, that the Italians themselves referred to as ''the French disease''. In such a way would Mazarin exclude any possibility of Orléans becoming a threat, or even a mere nuisance, to Louis' hold of power, as Louis XIII's brother Gaston had disrupted his reign. But in truth Philippe never wavered in his support of his brother Louis, and was ''privately in despair at his brother's illnesses, his loyalty total'' (38). For Louis' part, homosexual and bisexual men continued to be burned at the stake.

Mazarin awarded Philippe by making him captain-lieutenant over a new corps called the *Mousquetaires du Roi*, whose members were immortalized by Alexander Dumas's *The Three Musketeers*. Mazarin also left Philippe a part of his colossal wealth at the time of his death, passed on at *his* death to his six children, while another part of Mazarin's fortune went to Philippe's sister Hortense, whom Mazarin greatly favored.

## PHILIPPE D'ORLÉANS

It's difficult to know the reality of the relations between Louis and his brother Philippe d'Orléans, called *Monsieur* at court, but it is known that Louis respected him as the heir to the throne should something happen to Louis himself, in addition to Philippe's role as regent of Louis' son should Louis die. We do know that on Philippe's death Louis cried out, in pain, ''I don't know how to accept the fact that I shall never see my brother again!'' Louis disapproved of his brother's debauch and told Philippe so, Philippe who simply reminded the king of Louis' own mistresses, and reminded him that when he was younger he too, like Philippe, had had his way with any maiden that caught his fancy. Louis' ire fell on his brother's male lovers, lovers that Philippe's second wife--Elizabeth Charlotte, Madame Palatine, whom Louis called Liselotte [a melding of her names] and will be known in this book as Palatine--accused of acting as pimps for Philippe. Between the births of her children she claimed that Philippe ''permitted me to live in perfect chastity'', which she preferred to his pawing her, although she was furious with his ''lavish adoration of the Chevalier de Lorraine'' (38).

Philippe was Louis XIV's only heir until 1661. When his mother spoke of ''my little girl'', the court knew she meant her son Philippe.

Philippe had two wives, the first who stated that her husband's heart was ''reserved for no woman in the world'', and the second, Palatine, who wrote, in one of the 60,000 letters she bequeathed to us, that during a single winter Philippe had paid out 200,000 guilders to reward the men of the guards ''who entertained him in a not exactly honorable fashion.'' She went on to say that only the expense annoyed her, that otherwise he was ''free to enjoy those pleasures his age left him.''

One of Philippe's secondary lovers was Antoine Morel de Volonne, pictured here, of whom one biographer stated, ''He stole, he lied, he swore, was an atheist and sodomite and sold boys like horses'', while Saint-Simon added that he was ''soulless and lawless.''

About her husband, Palatine wrote that ''Monsieur has nothing in the world on his mind but his young boys, giving them unheard of sums of money, nothing too expensive for them.''

Saint-Simon wrote that ''Monsieur's tastes did not include women, and he did nothing to hide the fact.'' Taste, ''*goût*'', was also used when a man of 25, Primi Visconti [see Sources], was seen leaving the bedroom of the Marquis de La Vallière, the brother of one of Louis XIV's feminine favorites. Asked how someone as old as Visconti, with a beard, could be of interest to La Vallière, Visconti replied that ''a man of *goût* did not pay attention to either age or hair'' [Visconti at 25 was decidedly old in comparison to boys aged 14 to 18, the usual choice of men]. Visconti, a court historian who preferred women, later wrote that he couldn't refuse someone as important as the marquis, especially as the boy was young and handsome, Visconti claiming that he had known of La Vallière's intentions for a certain time, and had tried to avoid the inevitable.

That Philippe was only interested in boys and men is belied by the fact that he produced three surviving children with his first wife Henrietta of England [another stillborn and four miscarriages]. Her father was Charles I, Henrietta and her mother forced to flee England at the time of Charles's beheading (20), taken in by Louis XIV. Her mother, Henrietta Maria, was the daughter of Henry IV, and so she knew the French court well. Henrietta settled for Philippe when her mother's plans to marry her to Louis XIV fell through, Louis' marriage to Spain's Maria Theresa--now that Charles I was decapitated--deemed more favorable to France. Philippe's decision to marry Henrietta was enhanced when her brother became King Charles II of England and awarded her a dowry of 840,000 *livres* as well as 40,000 *livres* annually. Her first daughter was attributed to the works of Louis XIV himself, as well as the Count of Guiche, Philippe's lover, although Philippe himself may have been responsible, a perfect *panier de crabes*. Rumors of Henrietta's ''flirtations'' with Louis, Guiche and several other of Philippe's lovers, made Philippe jealous enough to poison her, or so court gossip had it, although the symptoms of her suffering have led modern experts to suspect she died of peritonitis, not poison. Philippe was also suspected of poisoning princes, no matter what the real cause of their deaths, in order for his son to one day become king. Thanks to Louis' daughter Françoise Marie de Bourbon's fertility, and the fertility of Philippe's daughters, the Bourbon bloodline spread throughout all of Europe, today's surviving kings, queens, princes and princesses all sharing a few drops.

Philippe was a military strategist and a man of courage, who made his brother Louis XIV so jealous that Louis cut short his military career after Philippe's first outstanding successes, and ordered Mazarin to give him money and to place him in the midst of young men on whom he could spend it, thereby keeping Philippe out of Louis' hair, but this may be pure speculation on the part of historians.

Philippe crossed-dressed, adorning himself with rings, earrings, bracelets, gems, his preference diamonds, ribbons and black, powdered wigs, curled to perfection. His face was rouged and a lover was at hand to apply the height of fashion, a black *mouche*--beauty spot, and the scents that masked a lack of baths, water feared to be a carrier of diseases, especially hot water that opened the pores to germs. His lover the Chevalier de Lorraine was universally described as beautiful and remained at Philippe's side for forty years, Philippe thought to have been age 11 at the time of their first meeting, the Chevalier 14, Philippe's taste for the Chevalier ''*durait depuis leur juenesse jusqu'à la fin de la vie de Monsieur*'', wrote Saint-Simon, a love affair in which the Chevalier ''hooked Monsieur like a harpooned whale'' stated historian Dirk Van der Cruysse, while Philippe's preference for sadomasochistic sexual diversions was met by the Marquis de Châtillon and the Comte de Guiche. Threesomes were favored, wrote Jonathan Spangler in a must-read 2007 article, *The Chevalier de Lorraine*, Spangler listing the Marquis d'Effiat, the Marquis de Beuvron and Charles d'Harcourt, captain of the Guard, as favorites, but in truth any number of boys and men, from pages to recruits to officers, would not have missed their chance at court advancement though intimacy with the brother of the king and the wealthy Chevalier, both men who had, in addition, proved their valor on the battlefield.

Saint-Simon wrote that Effiat ''was in full partnership with the Chevalier de Lorraine to govern Monsieur until his death, very often with insolence'', Effiat the darkest side to the court's reigning homosexual triumvirate which consisted of himself, the Chevalier and d'Orléans. Antoine II Coëffier de Ruzé, marquis Effiat was none other than the uncle of Cinq-Mars, the beheaded lover of Louis XIII, Cinq-Mars's father one of the lovers of Henry III, father and son basically, perhaps even entirely, heterosexual, but omnisexual when it was in their interest, while Antoine was an enthusiastic devotee to boys, whose ''little suppers'' could end in orgies, even though slipping off to a side room, or simply spending the night with one of the lads, was probably what took place most commonly, suppers that included not only Philippe d'Orléans but also Philippe's son Philippe II d'Orléans, although it is improbable that father and son were present at the same time. This was the major reason for Palatine's hatred of Effiat, and her uncertainty of just how far her husband would go to implicate his own boy in the most sordid aspects of court backroom indecency, especially when Philippe made it clear that he wanted Effiat named regent over the boy should Philippe die, forcing Palatine to go directly to Louis to lay out her case, stating ''This marquis is the most debauched fellow in the world, and particularly addicted to debauchery of the worst kind. If he becomes governor of my son, I can be sure that he will teach him what is the most horrible thing in the world.'' Louis, who immediately grasped the danger of putting young Philippe in the grasp of men like Effiat and the Chevalier, refused to give Effiat the regency, but by then it may already have been too late to protect young Philippe, especially if the boy, like Louis' son Vermandois, had already succumbed to the men's flattering ego-boosting, and sexually exciting, attention. Louis nonetheless lightened his refusal by allowing Effiat to found the Royal Military School, an adjunct to the Chevalier's School of Pages. Effiat had revenge of sorts by spreading the rumor that Palatine was welcoming lovers into her bed, which obliged her to defend honor, exclaiming to one and all that Effiat ''was the greatest sodomite in France.''

D'Effiat was one of those suspected of poisoning d'Orléans' first wife Henrietta, who loathed him as much for the vile acts she imagined he committed as for his effeminacy. Although her poisoning was unlikely, as discussed above, Saint-Simon nonetheless spoke of *how* Effiat poisoned her, stating that the poison had been put in Henrietta's personal *cup,* into which chicory water was poured, the chicory water itself free of poison for fear that others might be served at the same time.

Saint-Simon, who hated to touch on the subject of homosexuality, did so, discretely, in Effiat's case: ''Effiat lived as a bachelor, very rich, very inaccessible, very fond of hunting, and having access to Monsieur's pack [remnant of Frank Sinatra's Rat Pack], or on his estates almost alone, and seeing only obscure people, very particular, and obscure also in Paris, *with creatures of the same species*; rarely in good company for he was well off only with those who were common and complacent. He was a rather small man, lean, well-made, straight, clean, with a blond wig, with a reluctant mien, very glorious, polite with the world, and who had a strong language and demeanor'' adding elsewhere, ''You should know that the Marquis d'Effiat was a man of great wit and skill, who had neither soul nor principles, whose soul was Damned, who lived in a disorder of morals and public irreligion, equally rich and miserly. He governed Monsieur and the Chevalier de Lorraine, and ruled over his affairs with a baton, feared and admired for his mind'' [the emphasis my own]. Effiat had the use of eight rooms at Versailles and d'Orléans saw to it that Effiat was appointed to well-paying councils, abbeys, hospices and hospitals without ever having to show up. On his death, Palatine wrote, ''Yesterday an octogenarian died in Paris. May God forgive him for the harm he has done me during thirty years that I have lived with my lord. It is the Maquis d'Effiat.''

The Marquis de Châtillon was another of d'Orléans' sexual partners, d'Orléans' first Gentleman of the Chamber, whom d'Orléans made governor of Chartres and Knight of the Orders of the King. He was in the siege of Barcelona and Friborg, whose marriage, wrote Saint-Simon, was short-lived ''they fell out and separated, never to see each other again'', but highly amusing was Châtillon's brother, a member of the Royal Bodyguard, who complained to Louis XIV that Louis hadn't advanced his career as spectacularly as d'Orléans had helped that of his brother, to which Louis answered, ''One makes a fortune in my brother's service *by certain means* which would cause him to lose his favor if one were employed in mine'', my emphasis.

Palatine was depicted as being as masculine as Philippe was effeminate. She loved to hunt, for example, while Philippe made a harbor of tranquility of his Saint-Cloud forests where every animal could live out its life in peace. He did produce six children during his two marriages, as was the case of nearly all of his friends, despite their deeply homosexual natures. Palatine left behind 60,000 letters, as said, in one of which she wrote that the love that men felt for each other must be natural because Heracles, Theseus, Alexander the Great and Caesar were adepts, and that God had punished no one for sodomy since Sodom and Gomorra, now that the world had plenty of inhabitants. Sodomites had nevertheless to hide their love so as not to inflame the religious beliefs of the vulgar masses, she added.

Palatine described one of Philippe's nighttime activities: In bed, under covers, he seemed to manipulate himself, causing

Palatine, through curiosity, to fling back the covers, revealing Philippe rubbing his genitalia with a rosary and medals of the Virgin Mary. Philippe claimed that the practice protected his intimate parts from harm and assured his potency, but ''you, a Huguenot, certainly can't understand such things'' said he to Palatine, who replied that rubbing an image of the Virgin against the instrument meant to take a woman's virginity was not a way to honor Mary, to which Philippe reluctantly agreed.

In addition to his Versailles apartments, Philippe had two principle residences, the Château de Saint-Cloud with its gardens, woods and bushes for discrete couplings, secret niches behind waterfalls, caves, a veritable pleasure palace later destroyed by fire, and the Palais-Royal in Paris with its 169 paintings by Titian, Veronese and others, jewels and sculptures. It was Philippe who discovered Molière and his troop, in 1658, Molière just 18 and fully available to both sexes, the loves of his life a woman, Armande Béjart, and an adolescent, Michel Baron.

Jean-Baptiste Poquelin, known as Molière.

The Palais-Royal was built for Cardinal Richelieu and

bequeathed by the cardinal to Louis XIII, its arcades, cabarets and houses of pleasure highly appreciated by Cinq-Mars and his friends (39). Louis XIV passed it on to his homosexual brother the Duke of Orléans, after which it changed from a center of basically heterosexual activity to one more homosexually oriented, its gardens generously inseminated by nightly gatherings

Saint-Simon wrote that when Philippe died of apoplexy--during a dispute with his brother Louis XIV--all ''amusements, all pleasures, all soul, life and action'' at court died at the same time.

His wife Palatine took the passing in stride, her only concern the marriage contract that stipulated her entry into a nunnery should Philippe precede her in death, but she put up such a howl that Louis allowed her to stay in Versailles. She burned Philippe's love letters--a kind of what-happens-in-Versailles-stays-in-Versailles practice of the times--stating that the perfume they exuded nauseated her. She snuck into the palace's theatrical performances incognito, foregoing the conventional two years of mourning she refused to respect.

## THE CHEVALIER DE LORRAINE

The Chevalier de Lorraine, Philippe de Lorraine [1643-1702], was especially known as the lover of Monsieur, Louis XIV's brother. The Chevalier was a Grand Squire of France, and as such was known as Monsieur le Grand, a position we learned about in the life and times of Cinq-Mars, one that often put the owner [the position was purchased] in the king's bed, which is highly doubtful in this case, as Louis XIV appears to have been not only heterosexual, but also homophobic, and thusly not sexually attracted to the Chevalier [although historical scuttlebutt had Louis, Philippe and the Chevalier discover first-sex together at puberty, all three early companions, and later in life the Chevalier ''went into the king's chambers alone, after the *coucher*, and spoke with the king for some time in his bed, an action generally restricted to only the immediate royal family'' (44), which doesn't mean that something ''indecorous'' took place, although the Chevalier was truly a great beauty].

**Philippe de Lorraine, called the Chevalier de Lorraine.**

The Chevalier became Philippe's lover in 1658 at age 14, d'Orléans thought to have been three years younger, and was said to have been ''as beautiful as an angel.'' Omnisexual, he was the lover of Princess Henrietta, whose mother had taken refuge in France just before her husband, Charles I of England, was dethroned and decapitated. She was suspected of being poisoned by the Chevalier who wanted her out of his hair, or by her husband Philippe, jealous of her sexual congress with *his* lover the Chevalier, although everyone who died young at the time was said to have been poisoned because, due to court jealousies, nearly everyone had enemies. Poisoning was nonetheless rare, the truth being that fevers from diseases eventually carried nearly everyone off sooner or later.

Philippe was mad about the boy, so much so that even Louis XIV was worried about the Chevalier's influence. Both of Philippe's wives feared and detested him, and perhaps rightly so because the Chevalier was accused, as said, of poisoning the first, a continuation of the *panier de crabes* in that the Chevalier had been Philippe's first wife Henrietta's lover, she who married Philippe, the Chevalier's lover at the time. Philippe found a solution to the imbroglio by suggesting to Henrietta that the three unite in one bed (38), declaring that he could not love Henrietta ''unless his favorite is allowed to form a third in our union.''

The Chevalier seems to have had no saving qualities outside of his beauty, Dirk Van der Cruysse writing that he was ''rapacious as a vulture, without scruples, seductive and brutal.'' Historian Christine Pevitt called him ''utterly corrupt'', while author Nancy Nichols Barker wrote that ''he was athletic and had grace and beauty ... and a single-minded determination to make his way, ever conscious of his high birth and haughty in manner.'' He became so unsuitable that for a time Louis banned his presence in the same room, refused him any position within the court, and forbade his brother Philippe to offer him gifts. The Chevalier's outspoken complaints against Louis finally got him imprisoned under Louis' direct order in 1670, jailed in Lyon, then in the Mediterranean island fortress of Château d'If. Monsieur, furious, left the court for his holdings in Villers-Cotterets, taking Henrietta with him, knowing that this would cause Louis chagrin, a possible proof that Louis was intimate with her. As for Henrietta, she claimed she had been spared from Philippe mounting her, except on rare occasions, suggesting that their children were not his, her only concern: ''I fear the King may forget me'' (38). Away from court, Philippe could at least have presents brought to his lover in his imprisonment, ''caskets full of cash, jeweled garters, perfumes and gloves, shoes with lavishly expensive silver buckler'' (38), stating ''He is the best friend that I could have on earth and, being attached to me, languishes for the love of me [*amour de moi*] when he is not near me, I knowing better than anyone else the depths of his heart'', then pleading with Colbert to intervene with the king to give him the means ''to reconcile my fondness [*tendresse*] with my honor'', a quote brought to us by Jonathan Spangler. It's true that the Chevalier merited his place alongside Philippe, the Chevalier present at d'Orléans' *lever* since early boyhood, keeping him randy by ''speaking of young men in the way that a company of amorous boys has custom of speaking of young ladies'', making sure that said young men were in d'Orléans' grasp during the day and coming night. Added to this was Saint-Simon's insistence that the king showed little public affection for the Chevalier, while, at the same time, Saint-Simon was in awe that he ''enjoyed consideration, distinction and trust nearly as notable from the king as from Monsieur.''

It was perhaps to get Henrietta back close to him, as well as defuse his problems with Philippe, that Louis released the Chevalier, who exiled himself for a time in Italy where he could amuse himself with boys brought up in the Italian vice. Both the Chevalier and Philippe d'Orléans treated their wives as servants, Louis powerless to intervene because men's rights, in that domain, were incontestable, even by a king.

Historian Helmut Puff hit the nail on the head when he wrote that there was nothing unusual about omnisexuality (16) during the times, nor the numerous number of male and female sexual partners, that all was simply ''ordinary'', especially, underlines Puff, same-sex relations, a position backed up by researcher Allan Tulchin in what he called *affrèrement*, from the French word brothers, *frères,* mostly sexual but not necessarily so, an example Australian mateship (43) that was sexual in the absence of women during the founding of Australia, but not necessarily today.

Philippe gave the Chevalier rule over the Palais-Royal and the royal residence at Saint-Cloud, along with rooms at Versailles, while the Chevalier had family digs of his own, a palace at Frémont among them, where he entertained Philippe and the king. Everyone liked his company, his charm and immense good-looks, yet he was dreaded because all could feel the evil under the surface, the Abbé de Choisy writing that he was the ''Machiavelli of the antechamber.'' Even Philippe d'Orléans first wife, whom the Chevalier was later accused of aiding Philippe to poison, had called him an ''attractive rascal'' (44), while Madame de Sévigné [see Sources] wrote that ''he has a beautiful and open physiognomy which I love'', but also called him a genuine rake, not necessary an offense, the Chevalier's enemies certain he had pulled the wool over her eyes as he did many, one of them the Marquis de la Fare who described him as ''the most amiable and the most spiritual young man at court'' (44). Realizing that his looks would not last forever, he did his best to establish good relations with Louis XIV, this despite his having initiated Louis' brother into homosexual sex, as well as Louis' son Vermandois, his position in court aided by the fact that the Chevalier, thanks to his noble roots, was 16th in line for the throne, Louis a stickler for rank, thanks to which the Chevalier had been chosen as a playmate for Louis and his brother Philippe from boyhood. He was named the Grand Écuyer de France, with the title Monsieur le Grand, he was master of the stables, part of his job the direction of the king's School for Pages, an ideal nursery for his and Philippe d'Orléans physical needs. The fact that Louis knew that the Chevalier depended entirely on his favor, made him more trustworthy in Louis' eyes, the Chevalier at both brothers' sides for forty years. To establish his place in court as age set in, the Chevalier, wrote Primi Visconti, ''became a protector of *la belle jeunesse*, ensuring a steady supply of youths'' for the pleasure of court gentlemen. He had accumulated vast wealth throughout his lifetime and had produced illegitimate children, thanks to which the Lorraine line would continue on for still more generations.

Philippe d'Orléans and Philippe the Chevalier served together in military campaigns, d'Orléans, as Louis' brother, the commander, the high point of their careers taking place at the sieges of Zutphen, Turin and Cassel, as well as combat in Hungary and against the Dutch, the battlefield serving to weld their friendship and provide them with so many officers and recruits that Palatine wrote that the two Philippes' loves were ''were like dragon's teeth, a whole brood of fresh favorites that spring up to vex me'' (44), part of the reason for her displeasure concerning the money Philippe d'Orléans squandered on them, much of which was hers. Then, in 1682, Louis found out that the Chevalier was bedding Louis' own son, age 14, the Count of Vermandois, a lad shagged by numerous others and an enthusiastic participant in all-male orgies. The Chevalier was again exiled and Louis' son punished, although Louis didn't have the Chevalier beheaded in front of the boy, as Frederick the Great's father had had Frederick's lover Hans Hermann von Katte murdered, Frederick forced to watch (15). D'Orléans' courage at Cassel was reported like this to Queen Anne of England, painting D'Orléans clearly as homosexual: ''He does not lack bravery as was evident at Mont Cassel ... his affections do not go to women whose gallantry seems common to him, nonetheless he affects their manners … his make-up resembles the ladies more than a general of armies'' (44), and even Palatine claimed that he was brave, much more so than Louis XIV. Louis himself occasionally visited the pair on battlefields. He perhaps just tolerant of his brother's bent, perhaps believing, as did his Minister of War Louvois, that battlefield romances enforced cohesion among his troops and increased their valiancy, the men refusing to show weakness in front of their mates, an historical example the captured Theban soldier who entreated the enemy to thrust their sword into his chest and not his back, so that when he lover found him he would know he died valiantly.

The Chevalier passed away at age 59, a year after his lover, supposedly after a night of cavorting with prostitutes, these females--perhaps true, perhaps not, because heterosexual historians often try to give their subjects a heterosexual happy-ending.

''As beautiful as an angel'', stated his contemporaries.

## LOUIS DE BOURBON, COUNT OF VERMANDOIS

The dazzling hypocrisy and inhumanity of the court of Louis XIV is clearly seen in his treatment of his son, Louis de Bourbon, Count of Vermandois, born in 1667, six years after Louis' legitimate son by his queen Maria Theresa, Vermandois' mother the king's mistress Louise de La Vallière, who gave Louis two other boys that rapidly died. Louis legitimized Vermandois--described by Jean Loret, the court poet, as ''a living masterpiece''--and named him Admiral of France, at age two, which allowed Louis to have complete control over the French navy. Louis had sincerely and deeply loved Louise, a sin because he was committing adultery, Louis who was one of the most religious monarchs to have lived, never missing a mass, but was fortunate in having, for confessor since age 16, Jesuit Father Francois Annat, who showed great tolerance and understanding, his ultimate hope to bring the king back to the path of virtue, although rare is the priest who can impose piety over a male's penis.

Louis had declared Louise a royal mistress, a bizarre but recognized practice which made the liaison official and gave the mistress great power, a procedure Louis used only four times during a reign that lasted 72 years. But when Louis grew tired of Louise, whom he had been sincerely devoted to for a time, he used her in as cruel a fashion as any imaged by Molière in one of his misanthropic plays. She was ordered to share her residence with his new conquest, the Marquise of Montespan, a married woman, who eventually became the second of his official mistresses. Montespan's cohabitation with Louise was a smokescreen which allowed Louis to bed her, thusly avoiding upsetting Louis wife, Queen Maria Theresa of Austria, or dishonoring Montespan's husband, or highlighting behavior that some might consider scandalous [which it wasn't when declared official, wherein resides its bizarreness]. The humiliation was complete when Montespan treated Louise like a servant, Louise who decided to enter a convent as a way of publicly expiating her sins, her entry coinciding with Montespan's giving birth to one of Louis' adulterous bastards. Louise's vengeance was complete when, at the gates to the Carmelites, she begged the queen herself, Maria Theresa, for forgiveness.

As for Montespan's husband, Louis Henri de Pardaillan de Gondrin, Marquis de Montespan, he refused to enter the shadows of invisibility as husbands whose wives were ''honored'' by Louis universally did. He visited Paris's most infamous whorehouses in order to infect himself with syphilis he hoped to pass on to his wife who would then infect Louis; he donned his carriage with cuckold horns, declared his wife dead and forced his two children to attend her ''funeral''; he insulted the king in person in the gardens of Saint-Germain-en-Laye, for which Louis had him imprisoned for a short time; and he had an annual requiem sung for her.

Montespan gave Louis seven children, La Vallière five, Louis' wife Queen Maria Theresa six.

Vermandois was age 7 at the time his mother entered a convent, La Vallière apparently totally indifferent to the boy. He was placed with Louis XIV's blatantly homosexual brother Philippe d'Orléans and his wife, the extremely liberal-minded Palatine. Monsieur was one of the first to remark the evident homosexuality of Vermandois, and immediately set his handsome lover Philippe Chevalier de Lorraine to seduce the lad, perhaps itself a smokescreen for Philippe's own sexual access to the boy. By age 14 Vermandois was participating in orgies and was a member of a group formed by the two Philippes and others, the Holy Fraternity of Glorious Pederasts [*La Sainte Congrégation des Glorieux Pédérastes*], its meeting places taverns, brothels, townhouses and country residences, the orgies including guests and male prostitutes, with even women occasionally interspersed. The Marais region in Paris was favored by men seeking men, especially the Petite Rue des Marais where they gathered after the theater, the pretext the need to make water, the perfect excuse to fully show off their wares, ''concluding'' in alcoves in nearby pitch-dark alleys, while the gardens around Versailles, the Louvre and the Palais-Royal served the same purpose.

One of the major participants of *La Sainte Congrégation des Glorieux Pédérastes* was Roger de Rabutin, Comte de Bussy, who entered the army at age 16 and fought in several campaigns. Although he would later play an important role in the Holy Fraternity of Glorious Pederasts, and put forward a clause in the Fraternity's charter that forbade women, he was fully omnisexual, ordered to pay a huge indemnity to Madame de Miramion whom he had abducted for his sexual pleasure, Miramion rescued by order of the queen when it was learned that she was starving herself to death in preference to Rabutin's abuses, after which she entered a convent. He nonetheless spent a year in the Bastille and 17 years exiled to his estates.

Elected a member of the Académie française, he wrote his *Histoire amoureuse des Gaules*, written in the style of Petronius's *Satyricon*, published after his death because of his revelations concerning Versailles courtiers.

He is notorious for his organization of the Orgy of Roissy, having for participants Mazarin's nephew [some historians claim his son] Philippe Mancini, the Comte de Guiche and Louis Victor de Rochechouart, Duke of Vivonne, whose father had been a childhood playmate of Louis XIII and whose sister was Louis' mistress Madame de Montespan [who gave Louis seven children], Vivonne one of only six Marshals of France.

**Chosen as the First Gentleman of the King's Bedchamber, ''Monsieur de Vivonne had infinite spirit and entertained it without fear; he pleased the king with a hundred stories,'' wrote Saint-Simon.**

Louis accepted Monsieur's behavior because his travels throughout the hotspots of Paris and through the provinces in search of the lads he favored kept him too busy to plot against Louis as Gaston, Louis XIII's brother, had continually plotted against Louis XIII, although the real reason was probably just to keep him occupied outside of Versailles.

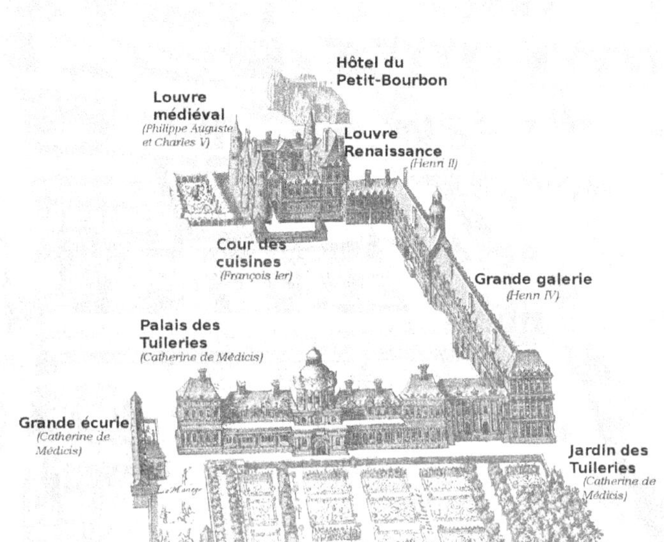



**The Tuileries around 1615. In the lower right-hand corner one can see the wooded area used for evening pleasures. Louis never entirely abandoned the Louvre for Versailles, the Louvre a second residence he continuously renovated.**

**Louis de Bourbon, Count of Vermandois**

When Louis found out the use the men at court were making of his own flesh and blood, he went wild with anger. He had the boy brought before him and flogged within an inch of his life. The lad was exiled, as were the participants in his debauch, including the Chevalier de Lorraine, but not Monsieur, the next in line to the throne after Vermandois.

It was Palatine who suggested to Louis XIV that the best way to reconcile himself with his son was to allow him to gain glory, after which Louis would be able to honorably welcome him back at court with open arms. Vermandois thusly headed troops that Louis sent to Flanders where he sieged Courtray. Alas, he came down with a fever, and wishing to not disappoint his father, he fought on despite his doctor's orders for him to rest, a decision that cost him his life at age 16.

When Louis XIV didn't as much as weep at the loss, as the court thought he would, he came out with this statement, ''It was at his birth that I should have wept.'' His mother showed even less sympathy when she learned of his death. Writers later placed Vermandois among the men who could possibly have been the Man in the Iron Mask, in reality a mask of black velvet cloth, an impossibility due to conflicting dates.

## PHILIPPE II, DUKE OF ORLÉANS

Philippe II, Duke of Orléans, was the son of the homosexual Philippe I. Philippe II was regent of France from 1674-1723, until Louis XV--Louis' successor [Louis XIV's great-grandson, then age 5]--reached his majority. Philippe allowed the printing of books banned by Louis XIV and acted in plays by Molière and Racine. In 1717 he bought the largest diamond known to man [141 carats], for £135,000 [26 million in today's pounds], and named it after his function, Le Régent.

To please his brother Louis XIV, Philippe I married his son Philippe II to Louis XIV's own legitimized daughter, a mismatch which had Philippe II calling her Madame Lucifer, although the marriage produced eight children, one of whom purportedly became her father's mistress.

Philippe I died during a dispute with his brother Louis XIV, who had not paid the immense dowry promised when Louis XIV's daughter married Philippe II, 2 million *livres* plus the Palais-Royal.

In 1722 12-year-old Louis XV was anointed King of France in the cathedral of Notre-Dame de Reims, after which he threw himself into the arms of Philippe II whom he felt had acted loyally during his regency. On Louis XV's majority, age 13, Philippe stepped down as regent. This took place on 17 February 1723, and on 2 December 1723 he died, greatly mourned by Louis XV. He was buried with French kings in the Basilica of Saint-Denis.

## THE CONFRÉRIE

Because no one could control the natural lust of men then, as today, frolicking continued within *La Sainte Congrégation des Glorieux Pédérastes* after the death of Orléans, now headed by Orléans's son Philippe II d'Orléans, the regent of Louis XV, and by Louis II de Condé, both wild participants in midnight debauch. Their bacchanalias (40) were known as the *confrérie* [fraternity], with a small ''c'' because we know so little about its foundation and rules, or even if there were any. We do know that it was a carbon-copy of an earlier *confrérie* of Italian inspiration, one centered around Versailles in the 1680s, that the Comte du Bussy-Rabutin, in his *Les intrigues amoureuses des rois de France*, claimed forbade sexual relations with women under the threat of exclusion, except if the man was obliged to marry because it was good for his affairs, or because his parents obliged him to do so, or because it was necessary in order to gain an inheritance, or if he needed a son, but the sexual relations to beget said son could take place only once a week and had to cease on the birth of a boy.

The 1722 version of the *confrérie* came to a momentary end when the Tuileries gardens were raided because the participants were becoming younger and younger. The leader of the *confrérie*, the Marquis de Rambures, was imprisoned in the Bastille and others were exiled. As the orgy and raid had taken place outside of the windows of Louis XV, age 12, the boy naturally asked what had happened and why so many nobles were sent away from court. He was told that they were guilty of digging up fences in the garden, and from then on fence-diggers became a euphemism for young homosexual gentlemen.

The meeting that decided the fates of the above sinners was presided over by homosexual Philippe II in person, who is said to have giggled throughout the entire proceedings but was forced to act in order to pacify the devout [both Philippe and Condé were atheists]. After sacrificing those he couldn't save, he and his friends waited a few months before reinitiating their nighttime activities. The Duke of Richelieu wrote this about the incident: ''The Regent, who did not stop smiling, was satisfied that it was necessary to give the nobles a harsh reprimand and tell them that they do not have the best taste in the world. Yet, when it was said that these gentlemen had formed a *confrérie*, he was obliged to call for their dissolution.''

Louis XIV had been informed about the orgies and the participation of his brother by his Minister of War Louvois, but was warned to drop the matter if he didn't want to gut and ruin the entire army!

## LOUIS JOSEPH DE BOURBON, DUC DE VENDÔME AND ALBERONI

Concerning Vendôme there are certain clarities: He was one of the greatest warriors of his time, his victories in Flanders, Italy and the Savoy, and domination over Spain so complete that he enabled his cousin to take power there as King Philip V of Spain, Vendôme himself chosen to succeed King Philip in the event of his childless death. A second clarity was his homosexuality, both open and without the slightest restraint, his Parisian mansion, in Paris's Place Vendôme, known as the Hôtel de Sodome, his pages and soldiers willing bed-fodder for the simple reason that his charisma attracted one and all. He was forced to marry at age 63, his wife unanimously described as ugly, which was not a holdback for Vendôme because he shared her immense wealth, never her sheets. Princes, dukes, princesses, counts and even the Dowager Princess of Conti were nonetheless present at the bedding ceremony, which in this case consisted of wishing the couple well before discretely exiting through one door while Vendôme immediately took French leave through another. In cases of royal alliances actual penetration had to be observed, the participants at the minimum the boy and girl's fathers, although their mothers and invited guests of rank were common. It was because no one had observed the penetration of Catherine of Aragon by Henry VIII's brother Arthur, Catherine later swearing that penetration hadn't taken place because Arthur had been ill, that the Catholic Church in England was replaced by the Anglican Church, Henry's request for a divorce based on his claim that she hadn't been a virgin when he married her.

Of Vendôme, Saint-Simon wrote: ''His valets and officers always satisfied his desires, his penchant well-known, and those seeking to win his patronage began by paying court to his favorites.'' An unnamed contemporary wrote: ''The peasant men of the environs of his fine property at Anet waited for him as he went out hunting, as he would often take them into the woods to fuck them, giving them a coin for their work, money that helped them pay their taxes.''

''Vendôme was of ordinary height, rather stout,'' wrote biographer Saint-Simon, ''but vigorous and active, his countenance noble and his mien lofty. There was much natural grace in his carriage and words, and he had a good deal of innate wit, supported by a natural boldness, which afterwards turned to the wildest audacity. He knew the world and the Court and was, above all things, an admirable courtier, polite when necessary, but insolent when he dared. As his rank rose and his favor increased, his obstinacy and pig-headedness increased too, so that he would listen to no advice whatever, and was inaccessible to all, except a small number of familiars and valets. He ordered his subalterns and those in his army to call him 'Monseigneur' and 'Your Highness'.'' Saint-Simon went on to state that ''the court accepted Vendôme's 'abominations' simply because the King did, the King who would never have pardoned a legitimate prince what he indulged so strangely in Vendôme.''

''Vendôme gobbled his breakfast and while he ate he listened and gave orders, many spectators always standing round. He supped copiously with his familiars, a great eater, even a wonder of gluttony. He shaved from the same basin he pissed in, stating that it was a simplicity dear to the Romans, and didn't hesitate to show himself naked to Alberoni, a priest.'' Saint-Simon went on to note his victories, stating that he commenced the Italian campaign by killing 3,000 men and taking 8,000 prisoners. ''Whereas there were other, great losses'' of his own men, concluded Saint-Simon, entirely due to ''the laziness and inattention of M. de Vendôme.''

Vendôme was popular among the men, their rise in rank assured for those chosen to plow the duke's belly, or if they brought him young recruits. One of his known lovers was Jules Alberoni, a boy who lost his father at age 10, earning his bread as a gardener, bell ringer and grave digger, whom visiting Jesuits taught to read and write and the rudiments of Latin, enough for him to be ordained a priest around age 25. He took up work in Rome where he learned French, the key to his future because he soon met up with Vendôme, who at the time commanded the French forces in Italy. Possessor of a lively and playful spirit, known for his ''low sycophancy'', wrote Saint-Simon, for whom no one was as filthily abject as Vendôme, who defecated in public and had his ass publicly wiped by servants, an ass that Alberoni exclaimed, when he first saw it, *''O culo di angelo!''*, greatly pleasing Vendôme. Dirty in the extreme, Vendôme slept with dogs, the females of which gave birth at his side, all of which apparently made him even more popular among the troops because he allowed them into his every intimacy, intimacy Vendôme shared with Alberoni who serviced the soldiers just as he was ''pleasing the principle valets'', wrote Saint-Simon. While Vendôme had been described as fat and ugly, Alberoni was noted as ''short and round in stature, an enormous head, a face of disproportionate breadth, a snub nose, lips that gave him a grotesque aspect, yet his gaze was noble, his elocution and voice enchanting, a man who worked 18 hours a day, as prideful as Vendôme and as vulgar, which, like Vendôme, endeared him to the common people, while in court he could instantly measure a man and the vices that would satisfy him, all to Albaroni's advantage. Because Vendôme was Marshal of France, everyone invited him everywhere'' stated Saint-Simon, who added that Vendôme was himself surprised at the sumptuous preparations and just how far the hosts were willing to go to grovel to his every desire.

All of which was nonetheless little in comparison to what the king himself was up to, Louis who had fallen for the beautiful eyes of Madame de Roquelaure, whose husband he sent off to war, most probably in the hope that he wouldn't return, outside of a casket, Roquelaure soon pregnant from his *oeuvres*, as the French call the art of impregnation. Vendôme presented Alberoni to Louis XIV who offered him a parish, which Alberoni turned down in order to follow Vendôme to Spain where Vendôme's cousin Philip V named Vendôme general. On Vendôme's death Alberoni had so ingratiated himself to Philip and the woman that Alberoni negotiated to become Philip's wife, Isabella Farnese, that he was given the powers of prime minister. States Saint-Simon: ''I have elsewhere alluded to Alberoni, and shown what filthy baseness he stooped to in order to curry favor with the infamous Duc de Vendome. Now Alberoni, unscrupulous and ambitious as ever, stopped at nothing in order to consolidate his power and pave the way for his future greatness. Having become prime minister, he kept the King as completely inaccessible to the courtiers as to the world. He allowed no one to approach him whose influence he in any way feared and had Philip completely in his own hands by means of the Queen.'' In fact, continued Saint-Simon, ''Alberoni had persuadêd the Queen of Spain to keep her husband shut up, the Queen his jailor and prisoner at the same time because as she was constantly with the King. Thus Alberoni kept them both shut up, with the key of their prison in his pocket.''

An incident took place which made it clear to Alberoni, who had been made a cardinal by then, that he couldn't keep the king in captivity for always: The Duc d'Escalone, called Marquis de Villena, insisted on seeing Philip. When a valet refused him entrance, ''the Marquis yellowed out, 'Insolent fellow, stand aside' and he pushed the door against the valet and entered. In front of him was the Queen, seated at the King's pillow, the Cardinal standing by her side. The Marquis, though full of pride, was weak in his legs and advanced supported upon his little stick. The King was too ill to notice anything, the curtains to his bed closed. Seeing the Marquis approach, the Cardinal made signs, with impatience, to one of the valets to tell him to go away, and immediately after, observing that the Marquis, without replying, still advanced, he went to him, explained to him that the King wished to be alone, and begged him to leave. 'That is not true', said the Marquis. 'I have watched you. You have not approached the bed and the King has said nothing to you.' The Cardinal insisted, without success, and took the Marquis by the arm to make him go. Stronger than his adversary, he turned the Marquis around and hauled him out. Calling Alberoni a 'little scoundrel' to whom he would teach manners, he raised his little stick and let it fall with all his force upon the Cardinal's ears and the shoulders, crying out that he deserved to be horsewhipped.'' With the help of a valet, the Marquis was ejected.

The writing clearly on the wall, Alberoni left for Rome in wild hopes of no less replacing Pope Innocent XIII who had just died, actually receiving ten votes. He became a legate of Ravenna in 1735 and of Bologna in 1740, and died wealthy in his palace at Plaisance in 1752.

Complaints against Vendôme eventually reached the ears of Louis, Vendôme's impertinences, obstinacy and insolence, his incapacity of judgment and his crudity. ''This was an opportunity for the ladies of the court, among them Madame de Maintenon and Madame de Bourgogne, to poison the king's ears concerning Vendôme.'' Vendôme was finally left with only ''his vices and his valets'', concluded Saint-Simon, who hated him for being a bastard and honored by men as they do their women.

He was finally brought low by the worst consequences of syphilis, punishment that many at court believed he fully merited given his ostentatious courting of youths. Mercury and other treatments led to his complete disfigurement, including the loss of his nose and teeth, his death at age 56 a form of salvation, as much from the pain of the disease as from Saint-Simon's hatred of him, Saint-Simon who detested bastards--Vendôme descended from a bastard son of Henry IV--and homosexuals, Saint-Simon conveniently forgetting the extreme importance of his father Claude de Rouvroy de Saint-Simon in the life and bed of Louis XIII (37), thanks to whose wealth Saint-Simon himself had lived in opulence and had received the finest education.

## PRINCE OF CONDÉ

Louis II de Bourbon, Prince of Condé [1621-1686], was also known as the Duc d'Enghien and, thanks to his military prowess, le Grand Condé [the Great Condé in English, but I'll continue with the French version]. His father saw to his excellent education and at age 17 felt confident enough in the boy's abilities to turn over the governance of Burgundy to him, while he went off to war. Alas, his father also forced him to marry a woman all found homely and dull, simply because the girl was vaguely related to the all-important Cardinal Richelieu. The marriage nonetheless produced three children.

Condé's victories throughout Europe were stunning, and with the death of his father he became one of the wealthiest men in France, inheriting the immensely prestigious title of *premier prince du sang*, which placed him in line for the throne itself, just after the son and grandson of the king.

Condé, through an extremely long career, found himself in a near-limitless number of battles, at one time fighting to save Paris, at another he fought to capture the city, at one time he fought against the Spanish, at another with the Spanish against his own French. He was even imprisoned by the regent, Louis XIV's mother, but saved thanks to the intervention of the homely wife he had disgraced in words and body. His wounds were legendary and in the Battle of Seneffe, against the Prince of Orange [later William III of England], he had three horses shot from under him.

He spent the last eleven years of his life in retirement in his Château de Chantilly, weakened from years of battle and sexual excess. He was omnisexual with a deep inclination for men and boys. Tallemant de Réaux, writer, memoirist and poet, was with Condé when he entered a tavern and, seeing *''un jeune garcon qu'il trouvait charmant, l'entraine dans sa chambre''* [''a charming youth, took him to his room.'']. Condé was dubbed the Great Masturbator because he loved to put his hand down men's trousers and bring them off while in conversation with them. *''Condé est un grand masterbateur qui met la main dans les chausses de tout homme qui lui plait.''* His favorites were his young pages, followed by recruits and his officers.

Another scene brought to us by Tallemant had Condé stopping at an inn where he met a charming schoolboy. He invited the lad to dinner and then to his room, a room that his lackeys immediately left because they knew the procedure well. Condé asked the boy if he and his school friends jerked off, and without waiting for a response he plunge his hand down the boy's pants and said, surprised, ''What! You don't have a hard-on?'' *''Il plonge sa main dans la culotte du chérubin. Comment? Vous ne bandez pas!''* Condé then took out his own dick and taught the boy how to jerk it with his left hand while introducing his right into Condé's ass *''et enseigne au novice à le branler de la main gauche en lui mettant les droits de la main droit dans le cul.''*

He died of rheumatism and, it was said, a life of exhausting sexual pleasure.

le Grand Condé and Condé with his son Louis III.

## PRINCE EUGENE OF SAVOY

In France and Italy at the time, the youngest son of noble families was reserved for the priesthood, an example Cesare Borgia, made a cardinal by his father Pope Alexander VI (23), but who realized his dream of a military career by murdering his older brother Juan Borgia (6). Such was the destiny also of Prince Eugene of Savoy, 1663-1736, born in Paris and brought up in the court of Louis XIV, preordained for the clergy, but was himself determined to enter the military, a decision rejected by King Louis due to the boy's poor physical bearing and Louis' physical relationship with Eugene's mother Olympia, one of Mazarin's nieces--Mazarin's Mazarinettes detailed in his chapter--Olympia who had gained the king's animosity by hounding him with her determination to become queen--as did the majority of Louis XIV's mistresses. His ambition thwarted at home, Eugene switched his loyalty to the Holy Roman Empire, moved to Austria and served three successive emperors. His victories, especially those against the Ottomans, won him glory, as did those against his native French, his reputation in Austria today unrivaled.

Like Louis XIII's mother, Olympia had little time for her children, her preference court intrigue, Eugene the youngest of five boys, brother of three sister, two of whom were said to have been as sexually dissolute at Eugene and their mother Olympia. We know, thanks to Princess Palatine's 60,000 letters, that Eugene was a dissipated sexually-promiscuous cross-dresser, small, effeminate, debauched, who ''was never good-looking'' ... ''a nose that ruined his face and two large teeth that are visible at all times,'' part of the reason why his decision to take up a military career had surprised his family and had been too ridiculous for Louis to even conceive. At the same time, Eugene's confidence in himself also exceeded reason, an example his arrogance when Louis had allowed him an audience, the Sun King later exclaiming, ''No one ever presumed to stare me down with such insolence'', Louis' decision to reject him, a rejection Louis would later regret when Eugen joined forces with English warrior the Duke of Marlborough, following which France went down in defeat after defeat.

Eugene and Marlborough, an unconquerable fellowship.

Eugene left us his memoirs--*The Memoirs of Prince Eugen, of Savoy*--in which he protested the exile of his mother, accused of sorcery and black magic, and, amusingly, stormed against the refusal of the clergy to accept him into its ranks, as originally planned, because Eugene, wrote Princess Palatine, was more ''shaped for pleasure than for piety''. Due to such insults Eugene ''swore I would never return to my country, except with arms in my hand, and I HAVE KEPT MY WORD.''

Eugene's hatred of Louis was transformed into adulation for

Holy Roman Emperor Leopold I, whom ''I promised to devote all my strength, all my courage, and if need be my last drop of blood.'' Victory after victory followed, Eugene just 22 when made a general but already so renowned that Frederick the Great's father sent Frederick to Eugene to learn strategy. Battles in Italy, Flanders, France and the Spanish Netherland so weakened France that Louis sent representatives to meet Eugene and Marlborough, but Louis found their demands so outrageous that he showed his steel by refusing them. Luckily, the arrival of Vendôme, Villars and other marshals in support of Louis, along with the menace of the Ottomans and political changes in England under Queen Anne and at the head of the Holy Roman Empire under Charles VI, reestablished France and Louis XIV as Europe's greatest power.

Only the advance of age slowed Eugene, who put his head on his pillow at age 72 for the last time, death making a fleeting, painless appearance in his sleep.

## PRINCE DE CONTI

Known as le Grand Conti due to his scandalous debauchery with both sexes (36), he was raised by le Grand Condé, his uncle, notorious for his unbridled homosexuality, but called Grand thanks to his military victories. Referred to as the Prince de Conti in court, François Louis de Bourbon-Conti, 1664-1709, married le Grand Condé's granddaughter with whom he had seven children. She was said to have been desperately in love with him, while he enjoyed his access to both sexes, one of whom was François Henri de Montorency, Duc de Luxembourg, at Conti's side when Conti enhanced his military reputation by winning the Battle of Steinkerque, two of Conti's horses shot from under him. Wounded in the Battle of Neerwinden, he was applauded by the court when he regained Versailles, the beds of one and all open to France's new hero. As he took an ardent interest in the women that Louis XIV felt were his own personal reserve, as well as Louis' daughter Louise Françoise, whose bed Conti frequently visited, Louis decided to get rid of him by paying the necessary bribes that got Conti named King of Poland, an elected monarchy. As few nobles wanted to rule a country as cold and a court as loutish as Poland's, Louis had to give Conti a stupendous 2,500,000 *livres* to make the trip to the forsaken northern wastelands. Yet he found, on arrival, that the throne had been seized by Augustus II of Saxony. In the same way that Henry IV had converted from Protestantism to Catholicism in order to be crowned King of France, King Augustus II converted from Protestantism to Catholicism to rule over Catholic Poland. During the voting to elect a new monarch Conti had received more votes than Augustus, but had tarried in luxury in Paris, during which time Augustus invaded Poland with his Saxon army. Deeply humiliated, Conti returned to Paris where Louis, vexed, encouraged him to regain his country estates and benefit from a rich retirement. Louis was nonetheless forced to recall him during the War of the Spanish Succession, thanks to Conti's military prowess, but Conti's services were cut short at age 45 when rich-food and bed-sports brought him death through gout and syphilis.

Conti, omnisexual and appreciated by both sexes.

## GUY ARMAND DE GRAMONT, COUNT OF GUICHE

Guy Armand de Gramont, Count of Guiche [1637-1673], was part and parcel of Louis XIV's brother Philippe's homosexual entourage, who brought Philippe's first wife Henrietta the sexual satisfaction lacking in her rapports with Philippe. Deemed the handsomest man at court [called the hottest guy at Versailles by one historian], his omnisexuality led him to bed women like Louise de La Vallière, Louis XIV's mistress, which got him exiled from court. He hired himself out as a kind of condottiere, fighting the Turks for Poland and combating the English when paid by the Dutch. Back in court in 1672, he joined Louis XIV and Guiche's homosexual friend the le Grand Condé in the Franco-Dutch war that saw Guiche swim across the Rhine at the head of a French army, an army spurned on by his example.

Dashing Guy Armand de Gramont, Count of Guiche, whom every woman and every man found sexually irresistible.
He was made a central figure in Dumas's novels *Twenty Years After* and *The Victomte de Bragelonne.*

## CLAUDE LOUIS HECTOR DE VILLARS

Claude Louis Hector de Villars--Prince de Martigues, Duc de Villars, Vicomte de Melun--was a man who led a life that was as much an ode to his military and political skills as were Louis XIV's own, Louis who spurred de Villars into action as Louis was doing his other generals in other battles, Louis' hand firmly in control, for it was Louis' will, determination and grasp of complicated situations that led to victory under seemingly impossible circumstance.

De Villars' military and diplomatic achievements won't be gone into in detail, but he was not only one of France's foremost marshals, he was a man who lived in the same conditions as his troops, eating the same food--or foregoing it in times of famine-- that made him stand out in the ways attributed to Frederick the Great (15), both of whom loved the men they commanded, and were loved in return, Voltaire who personally knew both and had even outed Frederick by publishing a list of his lovers, to Frederick's amusement, Voltaire the intimate friend of a huge number of homosexuals without, apparently, ever succumbing to the Italian vice. De Villars' love affairs were commented on in Princess Palatine's 60,000 letters, in which she also noted his appreciation of wealth and honors.

De Villars waged war until age 80, having begun his career as a page, the inexhaustible supply of boys since Emperors Trajan and Hadrian (32), then became a musketeer [and le Grand Condé's lover along the way], retiring as one of only six of France's generals to achieve the status of Marshal of France. He fathered a son, Honoré-Armand de Villars, born in 1702, a member of the Académie française founded by Richelieu and Louis XIII, a man so enamored of boys that he was known as ''*l'ami de l'homme*''. Honoré-Armand built one of the finest libraries in France, married into the wealthy and prestigious Noailles family, still another who could count on Voltaire visiting his estate, thanks to which Voltaire published his *La Pucelle d'Orléans* [*The Virgin of Orleans*], outing Villars as he had Frederick, and indicating that although Villars never had a child, his wife did behind his back, Honoré-Armand's reaction to Voltaire's disclosures unknown.

**Claude Louis Hector de Villars, Prince de Martigues, Duc de Villars, Vicomte de Melun.**

## DUC DE LUXEMBOURG

**Born a hunchback, François Henri de Montmorency, Duc de Luxembourg, 1628-1695, known as Luxembourg, was renowned for being the upholsterer of Notre Dame thanks to the flags from the countries he had defeated in war, flags that tapestried Paris's Notre Dame Cathedral. His father had been the valiant François de Montmorency-Bouteville (37), involved in so many duels that Louis XIII was obliged to put him to death, six months before the birth of Luxembourg. Luxembourg was taken into the Condé household by Charlotte Marguerite de Montmorency, Princess of Condé, and grew up alongside her son the Duke of Enghein, soon to be known as le Grand Condé, most probably Luxembourg's first love and lover. Luxembourg shared his sister, the Duchess of Châtillon, with Condé, Condé who repaid the favor by sponsoring the marriage of his cousin Madeleine de Luxembourg to Luxembourg, a further example of a French *panier de crabes*, everyone crawling over everyone else for standing, for advancement, for gains of every nature, like crabs, the least of which was sex.**

**Put in command of Louis' troops during the Franco-Dutch war [1672-1678] against the forces of Prince William III of Orange, he ordered the reduction to ashes of the town and**

garrison of Bodegraven, the inhabitants burned alive in their houses, a massacre he bragged about back in court, recounting to Louis how he'd roasted any Dutchman who crossed his path, surprised that some court nobles found such excesses horrifying. Louis, in recognition of his successes, made him one of only six Marshals of France.

Luxembourg at first kowtowed to Louis' Minister of War François-Michel le Tellier, Marquis de Louvois, known as Louvois, but following still more successes he felt himself powerful enough to quarrel with Louvois' decisions, while Louvois, far superior in the *panier de crabes* ins-and-outs of court intrigue, involved Luxembourg in the Affair of the Poisons, which landed Luxembourg in the Bastille.

The Affair of the Poisons, 1677-1682, *l'affaire des poisons* in French, was one of the major scandals in European history, ending with the executions of 36 people.

The affair had its origin in 1675 when a certain Madame de Brinvilliers was brought to trial for having attempted to poison her father and two of her brothers in order to inherit their estates, poisons thereafter referred to as ''inheritance powders''. She was beheaded after confessing under torture and her body was burned at the stake, her accomplice and lover having escaped judgement when he died of natural causes.

Nothing was more alarming than the possibility of being poisoned, a threat the Borgia used with amazing results in gaining and maintaining their power (6), a threat that Louis XIV immediately recognized as a way of getting to him despite the protection of his armies. So when another case of murder based on poisoning came to light--that of Magdalene de La Grange, Magdalene who, hoping to escape death, got word to Louis' Minister of War Louvois that she knew of plots against the king himself--Louis had his chief of police, Gabriel Nicolas de la Reynie, thoroughly look into it. Thorough was the key word because de la Reynie opened the investigation to include alchemists, witches, fortunetellers and even peddlers of aphrodisiacs whose white powders so resembled poisons. Under torture they all gave up names of others involved in any form of criminality, especially the names of their enemies, but one of them, a midwife, Catherine Deshayes Monvoisin, historically known as La Voisin, incriminated the most important of court nobles, from Olympia Mancini [covered in the chapter on Prince Eugene of Savoy] to Luxembourg to, incredibly, Madame de Montespan, Louis' chief mistress at the time.

Although the accusations against Montespan were the most fantastic, they were also the most credible because La Voisin accused her of buying aphrodisiacs she secretly administered to Louis, as well as performing black masses, the aim of both to encourage Louis to share her bed, while other substances and masses were aimed at her rivals, to lessen their importance in Louis' eyes.

La Voisin was burned at the stake and 34 people sentenced to death for poisoning and witchcraft, two others who died under torture, while 23 were exiled and five sentenced to the galleys, a fate worse than death. The exact number who died under torture and who committed suicide to avoid torture is not known. One of the exiles was Olympia Mancini, Countess of Soissons [whom we met in the chapter *The Court of Louis XIV*], one of the reasons-- along with his effeminacy--that barred her son Prince Eugene of Savoy's entry into the military, a decision Louis would later regret when Eugene fought against France, the story of which is found in his chapter.


Louis' need for unvanquished generals led to Luxembourg's release from prison, Louis' confidence in him justified by still more victories in the Spanish Netherlands. But the arrogance that had turned Louvois against him also earned Louis' disfavor when Luxembourg tried to wriggle himself to second in line to replace Louis at his death, manipulating royal claims and spurious lineage in his favor, supported by his adolescent lover Condé, the reality being that Luxembourg was 18th in line. Louis' disfavor didn't last long as Luxembourg fell ill and died, an apparently pleasant passage because the Jesuit priest who closed his eyes, Bourdaloue, said of his passing: ''I have not lived his life, but I would wish to die his death.'' Sexually immoral, the butcher of thousands, Saint-Simon summed up his life in this way: ''He had daring and confidence, and at the same time a cool-headedness that allowed him to observe and foresee in the midst of the fiercest cannonade, in dangerously critical moments. That was when he was truly great. At all other times he was idleness itself; no exercise, except where absolutely necessary; gambling; conversing with intimates; every night a small supper party; nearly always with the same company, and, if they happened to be near a town, an agreeable mingling of the sexes.''

## LULLY

Jean-Baptiste Lully, 1632-1687, was an Italian-born French-naturalized composer, his life spent in the court of Louis XIV, Lully who collaborated with Molière on the numerous ballets that adorned Molière's plays. At age fourteen Lully caught the attention of the Chevalier de Lorraine, residing in Florence, who saw the boy dressed as Harlequin during Mardi Gras, clowning about while playing the violin. Brought to Paris, he was seen dancing by Louis, the dance one of the king's favorite pastimes, who introduced him to Molière when the boy told him he could play instruments and choreography ballets. Lully produced his first opera at age 40, followed by 14 others.

He lost influence due to brazenly open homosexuality, said to have been incapable of keeping his hands off the boys he introduced as his ''students'', one of his affairs so flagrant that the boy's name has come down to us, Brunet, with whom he and Lully participated in the king's brother's orgies. He tried to regain the king's benevolence by celebrating Louis' recovery from an illness with a ballet of Lully's composition, during the repetition of which he wounded his toe so severely that gangrene set in, and when told that its amputation would ruin his dancing, he preferred death to surgery. His musical influence nonetheless continued in three of his composer sons.

## VERSAILLES

Historians strangely stumble over the hygiene at the time of Louis XIV at Versailles, one stating that he'd taken three baths during his entire life, another that he'd an octagonal bathtub, the size for two, sculpted from a single block of marble. The octagonal tub not only existed, but it can be seen in the Orangerie of Versailles, sculpted at the cost of an entire Parisian townhouse, made for Louis to pass some erotic moments with the person he shared it [although it had originally been created to please Madame de Montespan, Louis who complained that her abuse of perfumes turned his stomach, while Montespan answered that perfuming herself was the only way she could stand Louis' odor]. Louis had hundreds of orange trees, from which came the name Orangerie, their leaves believed to be aphrodisiacs. As stated before, the people at the time had good reason to not bathe, certain that warm water opened the pores to germs and all forms of diseases, a fear justified because water *did* carry diseases, typhoid, cholera, dysentery and, as far as some knew, syphilis, but the worst of all was the plague, a reason for the development of perfumes, thought to be weapons against it, Versailles known as ''the Perfumed Court''. At the outset of covid 19 people panicked too, as they did two-hundred years ago when Samuel-Auguste Tissot published a book in 1758 warning of the dire dangers of self-abuse, Tissot claiming that the loss of an ounce of semen equaled the loss of forty ounces of blood, a crippling factor that could lead to the loss of eyesight, to diseases and, due to increased blood flow to the brain, insanity, thusly condemning generations of boys to live in terror, one of the reasons why Spain spent a whopping €14,000 in 2009 on a campaign with the slogan ''Pleasure Is In Your Own Hands'' (29), aimed at promoting morning masturbation in the age category 14 to 17 as a way of lessening stress, a little like an apple a day... (42).

Louis himself had discovered the pleasure of baths in rivers, the moving unheated water deemed harmless. He also loved spas, where men could share stories about their nightly conquests of women. Bathtubs did exist, but the cost and procedure for filling them unwieldly, the water heated in kitchens and lugged through corridors to the tubs, tubs usually made of metal and lined with linen so the user wouldn't burn himself on the copper surface, the most famous example Jacques-Louis David's *Death of Murat*.

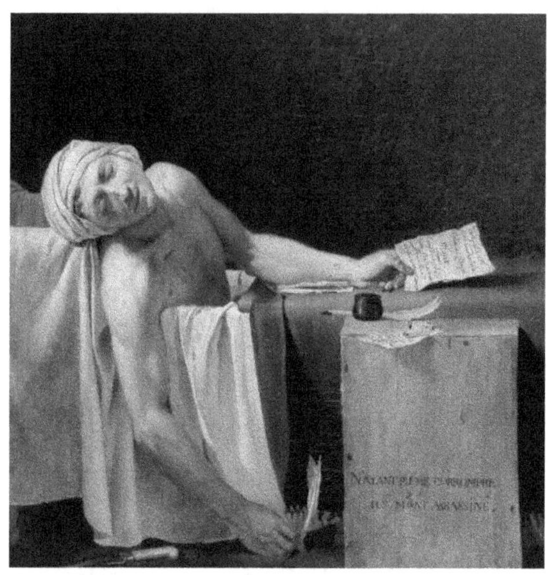

Murat in his last bath.

Scents took the place of baths, while exposed skin was rubbed clean with alcohol or fragrant substances, Louis himself given a daily full-body rubdown with alcohol because perfumes gave him headaches, the reason he didn't like to cloister himself in a carriage with scented courtiers. Interestingly, linen was considered a substance that cleaned the skin at least as thoroughly as water, and so shirts and bedding were often changed by those who could afford it, Louis who changed his shirt three times a day. Linen was hugely expensive at the time, and was the only underwear existent: a man, naked, put on his shirt in the mornings, which descended well into the trousers, completely covering the genitals and the buttocks, from which comes the commonly used expression in French *comme cul et chemise*, like ass-and-shirt, which means great familiarity, as in ''He says he's *comme cul et chemise* with his boss''. Trousers had flies, squares of cloth held in place by buttons on the upper right and left corners. Teeth were cleaned with powders for the purpose of making them look as white as possible, and mouthwashes were popular, the breath freshened with vinegar and wine mixed with honey. Clothes were washed and changed according to one's wealth, Louis' women in a position to own many outfits, the less rich forced to alter their daily appearance thanks to broches, laces and a variety of shawls. Airing clothing, especially robes, was the usual way of ''freshening'' them, and aromatic substances were burned in fireplaces. Bags were carried with good-smelling herbs and flower petals, some embroidered and extremely chic that one could bring to one's nose [in the way that it used to be chic for movie actors to bring cigarettes to their lips], and were also placed under arms.

At the time, the nobility thought of itself as being immanently clean, not only clean on the outside, but, thanks to bleedings, clean on the inside, for bleedings freed the body of foul humors, Louis bled at least once every two weeks.

Chamber pots were courtiers' toilets, carried through the corridors between their bedrooms and foul-smelling cesspits where servants emptied them, the odor lingering after their removal. The less wealthy emptied them from windows, the practice in Paris, the reason voyageurs stated they could smell the city before they saw the towers of Notre Dame. Kings and their entourages had to keep moving when they made their way around France due to the cost of nobles feeding them and the crushing amount of human wastes they left behind. Their horses too were responsible for mountains of excrement, from which comes the French expression for wishing good luck to actors, *Merde!* [''Break a leg'' in British English], because in those days playgoers drew up in front of theaters in horse-pulled carriages, the success of a play judged by the amount of horse manure left at the entrance, *merde* [shit] in French.

Boys and men often pissed off Versailles' balconies, stairways and balustrades, at times encouraging each other on, or simply against Versailles' tapestried walls. ''On the grand staircases and behind the doors and almost everywhere one sees there a mass of excrement, one smells a thousand unbearable stenches,'' stated an unknown courtier, water closets with runner water finally coming in with Louis XV. [When I first came to Paris in the '60s only half of the apartments had a bathroom, and for my first 10 years I had to wash in cold water (there was no hot), standing in a plastic basin in front of a sink. Deodorants, which I had used daily in the States, did not exist in Paris, with the exception of a pharmacy I finally found after weeks of searching, the Pharmacie Anglaise, but the product was so bad that it ruined my shirts by blackening the tissue. Today the first outlay of the French is a sumptuous bathroom, and in each supermarket there are rows and rows of deodorants. (7)]

Voltaire called the latrines in Versailles ''smelling shitholes'' and commodes--pierced chairs--were located behind screens in corridors for those who couldn't make it back to the chamber pots and *chaises percées* in their rooms, or to the several latrines located around the Versailles grounds. Hay, leaves and cloth were used for wiping.

Louis commissioned the creation of a new scent each week for his Perfumed Court, his shirts scented with nutmeg, balsam, cloves, rosewater, jasmine, lavender, sandalwood, vanilla and orange-flower water, while musk was added to the apparel of the more daring, especially men seeking their kind, and the Prince of Condé had his snuff fragranced. Louis had thousands of acres of land dedicated to the production of flowers at Montpellier and Grasse, the magnificently beautiful flower-blanketed hills of Grasse world-famous to this day, from which came two of Louis' favorites, Aqua Angeli and Aqua Mirabilis. The profession of perfume peddlers was bustling, especially bellowing the merits of their wares in the streets of Paris.

## LE PALAIS-ROYAL

The Palais-Royal was built by Richelieu in 1627, who offered it to Louis XIII at Richelieu's death in 1642. It consisted of Richelieu's palace and gardens, and over time shops and arcades were built to shelter restaurants, cafés and gambling houses, eventually becoming a center of prostitutes of both sexes, pickpockets and pimps who specialized in blackmail. It was the perfect meeting and mixing place of the high- and low-born, and drew so many political dissenters that it became known as the home of the French Revolution. A temple of sensual pleasure, it was later described in New York newspapers as being worse than Central Park. The ambassador of Constantinople wrote that during the time of Napoleon rooms above the shops were offered for debauchery, furnishing 1,500 boys and an equal number of girls to clients, from ages 12 upwards, although those found in *flagrante delicto* were hauled away by the police. During the 1840s cabarets (17) made their appearance, with private rooms, bad wine and inflated prices.

The commerce of bodies was accepted in the time of Richelieu, Louis XIII and Louis' lover Cinq-Mars, Cinq-Mars a heterosexual who liked to take girls to the Palais-Royal or go there with male friends to participate in bacchanalias (39). Philippe d'Orléans turned over apartments in the Palais-Royal to the Chevalier de Lorraine, the building later given to the Chevalier by Philippe d'Orléans' son Philippe II d'Orléans, Philippe II stating that he had received his wealth from his father, so ''it will always be him who gives it to you.'' A hundred years later the Palais-Royal had become vulgar and disreputable, the boys signaling their availability through gestures with hands and tongues, displaying themselves at urinals or while pissing against walls, dropping to their knees in the bushes if not invited to rooms in specialized houses or cafés and above cabarets, or the private chambers in restaurants, favored by Proust (31).

Laborers could earn money by turning tricks, some for pocket change, others who left their jobs in favor of nights of well-paid libertinage and days in their beds, in place of hard labor on factory floors. A good number of domestic servants added to their wages through prostitution, as did clerks, tailors and soldiers [while in London and Berlin the trade outside of barracks brought in large sums for soldiers and sailors, and was safe for the clients because military personnel rarely turned to blackmail and were kept clean by barrack doctors (27)]. Londoners, and especially Germans, liked their boys masculine, and lads in lederhosen could show off their tanned and muscular thighs, the inner pockets cut away so the john could introduce his hand and pulp the merchandise (15). The French liked more effeminate types who were soft and wore tight-fitting trousers (31).

Later the Palais-Royal had fairs, arcades with coin-operated attractions and cinemas, and was the preferred hunting grounds of the likes of Gide and Montherlant (41), while in other parts of Paris the opera and theaters were reserved for the educated set, sex taking place in the lodges, accompanied by the sound of zippers going up at intermission in the standing-room sections, followed by cruising in parks and gardens, especially on the grounds of the Louvre and the bushes of Notre Dame, to which can be added, today, the woods surrounding the Eiffel Tower and the Sacré Coeur.

## LE LOUVRE

Founded by Philippe II--the lover of Richard Coeur de Lion (37 and 41)--the Louvre became a royal residence under François I. Named in Roman times after the Latin lupara, meaning wolf [wolves frequent then], Louis XIV used it as his palace until moving to Versailles, the Louvre becoming a museum as a consequence of the French Revolution. The art collection increased so dynamically under Napoleon that the museum was called the Musée Napoléon until his abdication. In the early 1800s it was opened to the public four hours a week, expanded to Sundays and holidays in 1824, free until 1922. The most visited museum in the world today, the number of entries exploded after the building of Pei's pyramid.

The Louvre today and during the lifetime of Louis XIV.

## FONTAINEBLEAU

Located 35 miles [56 kilometers] from Paris, Fontainebleau was the hunting ledge of Louis VII, where Philippe le Bel was born and died, and François I invited the masterful Cellini (1) for a sojourn, François who genuinely put sodomists to death but was forced to accept Cellini, his boys and his carousing through the streets of Paris (1). Louis signed the Edict of Fontainebleau there in 1685 that gave Huguenots the choice between converting to

Catholicism, exile or death.

Henry III was born at Fontainebleau in 1574, as was Louis XIV's first legitimate son; Molière wrote his *Tartuffe* on the premises; and Aaron Copland, homosexual composer of *Rodeo, Billy the Kid* and *Appalachian Spring,* graduated from the Fontainebleau School of Music in 1921.

The woods around the palace were well-known for their sexual activity, then as they are today.

Louis XIV used Fontainebleau as a hunting lodge where he resided every autumn of his life. The exiled Queen of Sweden, Christina [her life portrayed in the Rouben Mamoulian masterpiece *Queen Christina* that immortalized Garbo] stayed there. She justified her reputation as the Swedish Amazon by having a former lover, the Marquis Monaldeschi, hacked to death in Fontainebleau's famous Gallery, and although she tried to wash away the traces, enough were left to shock Louis and his entourage during their autumn visit.

## SOURCES

## SOURCES DURING THE TIME OF LOUIS XIII

Héroard (pronounced Hérouard) was a very professional doctor, son of a surgeon, born in Montpellier, the site of the best medical education in France, then as today. At first he was Charles IX's veterinarian, but was then appointed Henry III's doctor and was present at Henry's autopsy after his assassination by Clément. Named Henry IV's doctor, he changed his faith from Protestant to Catholic when Henry did so. At age 50 Henry gave him the sacred trust of the future Louis XIII. Héroard kept a daily *Journal*, 11,000 pages over 27 years, until he died at age 78. Louis was extremely affected by his death, and soon followed his illustrious friend. 6% of his *Journal*, the picturesque parts, was published in 1868, while the scientific parts came out in 1989. He also wrote a superb book on horse bone structure, called *Hippostologie.*

Montglat (François de Clermont de Montglat): He is known for his *Mémoires* which recounted the wars between France and the Holy Roman Empire. He was himself a soldier and wounded. He was Louis III's head valet and served Louis XIV. His *Mémoires* were published after his death in 1727 at age 67.

Primi Visconti--an aka for Jean-Baptiste Primi Visconti Fassola de Rasa, 1648-1713--was an Italian writer, chronicler and historian of the court of Louis XIV, his chief work *Memoirs on the court of Louis XIV, 1673-1681*. He closely followed the Affair of the Poisons and the Dutch War, his book on latter landing him in the Bastille. He returned home but, accused of too ardently defending French interests, he escaped to Paris where he married a wealthy widow and spent his last years in luxury.

Princess Palatine--Elizabeth Charlotte, Madame Palatine, 1652-1722--was a German member of the House of Wittelsback, the wife of Philippe I, Duke of Orléans, the younger homosexual brother of Louis XIV. Where her husband was effeminate, Palatine was manly, her chief love the hunt.

Philippe ended his sexual relations with her after the birth of three children, to the relief of both. Louis XIV was very fond of her, and said she was the only one at court who appreciated the beauty of the parks around Versailles, due to her long nightly walks, while the court laughed because they knew of what purpose the parks were used after dark, although most probably Palatine just turned her head if she saw something amiss. One of her sons died at age three, attributed to bloodletting by family doctors, while her son Philippe was believed by many at court to have caused the deaths of the heirs to Louis' throne through poisoning and accidents of various kinds so that he himself would become king, rumors that ended when he became Louis XV's regent and allowed the boy to live.

Richelieu's *Mémoires* were compiled after his death by his faithful servants.

Rochefoucauld (La) is considered an example of the very finest in French nobility, having mastered court etiquette and oratorical elegance. Married at age 15, a soldier at 16, he was shot in the head during a battle but survived. An integral part of plots during the reigns of Louis XIII and Louis XIV, he was checkmated first by Richelieu, then by Mazarin. His *Mémoires* were pieced together by others and perhaps consist of only 1/3$^{rd}$ of his personal work. He later denied their authenticity. Politics for him were based on power moves by the greats, not ideologies or philosophies. He was said to have been morally scrupulous, which didn't stop him from taking as mistress the wives of others. Interestingly, he was introduced into Louis' court by none other than the ubiquitous Madame de Chevreuse!

Saint-Simon--Louis de Rouvroy, duc de Saint-Simon, 1675-1755--was a memoirist who has offered us the liveliest, most complete account of the reign of Louis XIV. Born when his father was 68, Louis XIV and Queen Maria-Theresa were his godparents. He joined the Mousquetaires, his youth dedicated to fighting for the crown, but left military service to take up a career in writing, his aim to enlist the help of courtiers, nobles and valets in discovering what was going on backstage in Versailles, and then relating it unpolished in his *Mémoires*, including his loathing of court ''bastards'' and homosexuals, certainly aware that his father had been the jewel of Louis XIII's boys (37), his own relationship with homosexual Louis II d'Orléans known to have been intimate[but not *how* intimate]. Of his style of living, it is said he went through the entire wealth left to him by his father, as well as what he'd earned on his own, the perfect end of what must have been an eventful life.

**Claude de Rouvroy de Saint-Simon, the memoirist's dad, of unparalleled beauty.**


**Sévigné, Madame de--her full name Marie de Rabutin-Chantel, marquise de Sévigné--was, like Palatine, known for the letters she wrote to her daughter. From a noble family, she married into wealth, her husband killed during a duel over his mistress. She knew many nobles, her favorite La Rochefoucauld, from whom she gleaned indirect information about court people and events. After her death her letters were passed to her granddaughter who saw to their publication, editing out family matters and rewriting sections. Her letters are featured in Proust's *In Search of Lost Time* because they were read by Proust's mother.**


**Tallemant (Gédéon Tallemant des Réaux): Born a Protestant in La Rochelle, he came into financial ease by wedding Elisabeth de Rambouillet whose mother Madame de Rambouillet hated Louis XIII and filled the young Tallemant's head with stories from the courts of Henry IV and Louis XIII, stories proved true by multiple sources and of huge historical interest. Tallemant put them together--along with his own research--in his best known work, *Historiettes*. He died a converted Catholic in Paris in 1692 at age 73. Catherine de Vivonne, Marquise de Rambouillet, Elisabeth's mother (called simply Madame de Rambouillet) had been beautiful when young, genuinely kind, and a woman who lacked all prejudices, opening her salon to literary figures--**

thereby advancing their careers--as well as nobles and actors. Molière wrote his chef-d'oeuvre *Les Précieuses ridicules* on the salons inspired by Rambouillet's salon, cheap salons compared to the original, but hysterically funny imitations.

Vittorio Siri: Born in Parma Italy in 1608, he became a professor of mathematics in Venice and was introduced into politics by the French ambassador who befriended him. When he began to write history, in favor of France, Richelieu gave him access to his archives, and later Mazarin offered him a pension.

## OTHER SOURCES

(1)  See my book *Cellini.*

(2)  See my book *Renaissance Murderers.*

(3)  Far more detail in my book *Henry III.*

(4)  See my book *Homosexual Heroes.*

(5)  See my book *TROY* or, in the coffee-table-size edition, *The Trojan War.*

(6)  See my book *Cesare Borgia.*

(7)  See my autobiography *Michael Hone His World, His Loves.*

(8)  See my book *The World's Most Fabulous Men.*

(9)  See my book *Renaissance Homosexuality.*

(10)  See my book *Caravaggio.*

(11)  See my book *Five Renaissance Wonders.*

(12)  See my book *Bartholomew Massacres.*

(13)  See my book *Florence.*

(14)  See Philippe Erlanger's *The King's Minion: Richelieu, Louis XIII, and the Affair of Cinq Mars.*

(15)  See my book *German Homosexuality.*

(16)  See my book *Omnisexuality.*

(17)  See my book *The Belle Epoque.*

(18)  See my book *Love The Gay Way.*

(19)  See my book *Hollywood's Homosexual History.*

(20)  See my book *Buckingham.*

(21)  Jean-Christian Petitfils's *Louis XIII.*

(22)  See my book *Julius II.*

(23) See my book *Alexander VI*.

(24) See my book *Greek Homosexuality*.

(25) See my book *Roman Homosexuality*.

(26) See my book *Exploration Giants*.

(27) See my book *The History of British Homosexuality*.

(28) See my book *Alexander & Hephaestion*.

(29) See my book Male Self-Pleasuring.

(30) George de Schomberg whose brother Gaspard de Schomberg became the father of Louis XIII's Marshal of France Charles de Schomberg.

(31) See my book *French Homosexuality*.

(32) See my book *Hadrian and Antinous*.

(33) See Ian Dunlop's *Louis XIV*.

(34) From Philippe de Dangeau's *Journal*.

(35) From Jerome Blum's *The European World*, 1970.

(36) Wikipedia *François Louis, Prince of Conti*.

(37) See my books *Louis XIII*.

(38) A quote taken from Antonia Fraser's *Love and Louis XIV*.

(39) See my book *Cinq-Mars*.

(40) See my book *The History of Orgies*.

(41) See my book *French Homosexuality*.

(42) See my book *Phallus*.

(43) See my book *The Homosexual History of Australia*.

(44) From Jonathan Spangler's *The Society of Princes*.


Aldrich and Wotherspoon, *Who's Who in Gay and Lesbian History,* 2001.

Aronson, Marc, *Sir Walter Ralegh*, 2000.

Baglione, *Caravaggio*, circa 1600.

Barber, Richard, *The Devil's Crown--Henri II and Sons*, 1978.

Barker, Nancy Nichols, *Brother to the Sun King*, 1989.

Bellori, *Caravaggio*, circa 1600.

Bergreen, Laurence, *Over the Edge of the World. Magellan.* 2003.

Blanchard, Jean-Vincent, *Éminence, Cardinal Richelieu and the Rise of France* 2011. Excellent!

Boyd, Douglas, *April Queen*, 2004.

Bluche, François, *Louis XIV*, 1986.

Blum, Jerome, *The European World*, 1970.

Calimach, Andrew, *Lover's Legends*, 2002.

Cawthorne, Nigel, *Sex Lives of the Popes*, 1996

Cellini, Benvenuto, *The Autobiography of Benvenuto Cellini.*

Crompton, Louis, *Homosexuality and Civilization*, 2003.

Crowley, Roger, *Empires of the Sea*, 2008. Marvelous.

Cruysse, Dirk Van der, *Louis XIV*, 1991.

Davidson, James, *Courtesans and Fishcakes*, 1998.

Davis, John Paul, *The Gothic King, Henri III*, 2013.

Dunlop, Ian, *Louis XIV*, 2000.

Erlanger, Philippe, *The King's Minion*, 1901.

Frieda, Leonie, *Catherine de Medici*, 2003. Wonderful.

Fraser, Antonia, Love and Louis XIV, 2006.

Graham-Dixon, Andrew, *Caravaggio* 2010. Fabulous.

Grazia, Sebastian de, *Machiavelli in Hell*, 1989.

Guicciardini, *Storie fiorentine (History of Florence)*, 1509.

Halperin David M. *One Hundred Years of Homosexuality*, 1990.

Hibbert, Christopher, *Florence, the Biography of a City*, 1993.

Hibbert, Christopher, *The Borgias and Their Enemies*, 2009.

Hibbert, Christopher, *The Rise and Fall of the House of Medici*, 1974.

Hicks, Michael, *Richard III*, 2000.

Hine, Daryl, *Puerilities*, 2001.

Hughes-Hallett, *Heroes*, 2004.

Hutchinson, Robert, *House of Treason*, 2009.

Hutchinson, Robert, *Thomas Cromwell*, 2007.

Lacey, Robert, *Henry VIII*, 1972.

Lambert, Gilles *Caravaggio*, 2007.

Landucci, Luca, *A Florentine Diary*, around 1500, a vital source.

Lev, Elizabeth, *The Tigress of Forli*, 2011. Wonderfully written.

Levy, Buddy, *Conquistador*, 2009

Lubkin, Gregory, *A Renaissance Court*, 1994.

Lyons, Mathew, *The Favourite*, 2011.

Mallett, Michael and Christine Shaw, *The Italian Wars 1494-1559*.

Manchester, William, *A World Lit Only By Fire*, 1993.

Mancini, *Caravaggio*, circa 1600.

McLynn, Frank, *Richard and John, Kings of War*, 2007. Fabulous.

Meyer, G.J. *The Borgias, The Hidden History*, 2013.

Miller, David, *Richard the Lionheart*, 2003.

Moote, Lloyd, *Louis XIII, The Just*, 1989.

Mortimer, Ian, 1415, *Henri V's Year of Glory*, 2009.

Noel, Gerard, *The Renaissance Popes*, 2006.

Parker, Derek, *Cellini*, 2003, the book is beautifully written.

Pascal, Jean Claude, *L'Amant du Roi*, 1991.

Pernot, Michel, *Henri III*, Le Roi Décrié, 2013, Excellent book.

Petitfils, Jean-Christian, *Louis XIII*, 2008, wonderful.

Pevitt, Chrtinse, Philippe, *The Man Who Would Be King*, 1997.

Puff, Helmut, *After The History of Sexuality*, 2012.

Read, Piers Paul, *The Templars*, 1999.

Reston, James, *Warriors of God, Richard and the Crusades*, 2001.

Ridley, Jasper, *The Tudor Age*, 1998.

Robb, Peter, *Street Fight in Naples*, 2010.

Rocke, Michael, *Forbidden Friendships*, 1996. Fabulous/indispensible.

Ross, Charles, *Richard III*, 1981.

Sabatini, Rafael, *The Life of Cesare Borgia*, 1920.

Saslow, James, *Ganymede in the Renaissance*, 1986.

Simonetta, Marcello, *The Montefeltro Conspiracy*, 2008. Wonderful.

Skidmore, Chris, *Death and the Virgin*, 2010.

Solnon, Jean-Fançois, *Henri III*, 1996.

Spangler, Jonathan, *The Society of Princes*, 2009.

Strathern, Paul, *The Medici, Godfathers of the Renaissance*, 2003. Superb.

Tulchin, Allan, *Same-Sex Couples*, 2007.

Unger Miles, *Magnifico, The Brilliant Life and Violent Times*

Unger, Miles, *Machiavelli*, 2008.

Vernant, Jean-Pierre, *Mortals and Immortals*, 1991.

Viroli, Maurizio, *Niccolo's Smile, A Biography of Machiavelli*, 1998.

Warren, W.L., *Henri II*, 1973.

Weir, Alison, *Eleanor of Aquitaine*, 1999. Weir is a fabulous writer.

Wikipedia: Research today is impossible without the aid of this monument.

Wilson, Derek, *The Uncrowned Kings of England*, 2005.

**Wright, Ed, *History's Greatest Scandals*, 2006.**

**I've priced my autobiography, *Michael Hone His World, His Loves*, at the lowest cost permitted by the editor.**

**I would also like to introduce what I consider my best book: *TROY* and its large coffee-table-size edition *The Trojan War*.**